Day *by* Day
with Pope Francis

The Word Among Us Stand-Up Calendar

Compiled by Jeanne Kun

the**WORD**
among us®
Press

SAINT SYLVESTER I

May the Mother of God, in whose name tomorrow we begin a new phase of our earthly pilgrimage, teach us to welcome God made man so that every year, every month, every day may be filled with his eternal Love. So be it!

—Homily, St. Peter's Basilica, Celebration of First Vespers of the Solemnity of Mary, Mother of God, December 31, 2013

DECEMBER 31

ISBN: 978-1-59325-274-8

Printed and bound in China

Cover design by Andrea Alvarez

Photo credit: Getty Images

Jesus, Mary, and Joseph, in you we contemplate the splendor of true love, to you we turn with trust. Holy Family of Nazareth, grant that our families too may be places of communion and prayer, authentic schools of the Gospel, and small domestic Churches.

—Prayer to the Holy Family during Angelus Address,
St. Peter's Square, December 29, 2013

DECEMBER 30

Introduction

Those who know Jesus, encounter him personally, are captivated, attracted by so much goodness, so much truth, so much beauty, and all with great humility and simplicity. To seek Jesus, to find Jesus: this is the great treasure!

—Angelus Address, St. Peter's Square, July 27, 2014

Since his election in 2013, Pope Francis has touched and captured the hearts of men and women all around the world—Christians and unbelievers alike. With loving warmth, bracing candor, and gentle humor, he reassures us of God's infinite mercy, challenges us to recognize Jesus in the daily circumstances of life, and encourages us to reach out to others in generosity and kindness.

Day by Day with Pope Francis features selections from the homilies, public addresses, letters, and other writings of the Holy Father addressed to the world since

SAINT THOMAS BECKET

Let us give thanks for all the blessings which God has bestowed on us, especially for his patience and his faithfulness, which are manifest over the course of time but in a singular way in the fullness of time, when "God sent forth his Son, born of woman" (Galatians 4:4).

—Homily, St. Peter's Basilica, Celebration of First Vespers of the Solemnity of Mary, Mother of God, December 31, 2013

DECEMBER 29

the beginning of his papacy. These quotations offer words of hope, comfort, inspiration, courage, and incentive. Embracing God's forgiveness, trusting in the Father's love for us, following Jesus on the path of discipleship, opening our hearts to the Lord's "surprises" and the work of the Holy Spirit, exercising charity toward our neighbor, proclaiming the Gospel with joy, fostering unity among Christians—these are among the themes that the pope repeatedly emphasizes and calls us to take to heart.

Designed to be used year after year, this compact stand-up calendar fits conveniently on your desk, bedside table, or kitchen counter. As you turn its pages day by day, may you "enter into true friendship with Jesus, so that following him closely, you may live with and for him" (Pope Francis, May 29, 2014).

Jeanne Kun
The Word Among Us Press

HOLY INNOCENTS

Let us . . . entrust ourselves to Mary, that she as mother of our firstborn brother, Jesus, may teach us to have the same maternal spirit toward our brothers and sisters, with the sincere capacity to welcome, to forgive, to give strength, and to instill trust and hope. This is what a mother does.

—General Audience, St. Peter's Square, September 3, 2014

DECEMBER 28

BLESSED VIRGIN MARY, THE HOLY MOTHER OF GOD

May Mary, the Mother of God and our tender Mother, support us always, that we may remain faithful to our Christian vocation and be able to realize the aspiration for justice and peace that we carry within us at the start of this new year.

—Angelus Address, St. Peter's Square, January 5, 2014

JANUARY 1

Saint John, Apostle and Evangelist

Saint John, the disciple who stood with Mary beneath the cross, brings us to the sources of faith and charity, to the heart of the God who "is love" (1 John 4:8, 16). He reminds us that we cannot love God if we do not love our brothers and sisters.

—Message for the 22nd World Day of the Sick 2014

DECEMBER 27

SAINTS BASIL THE GREAT AND GREGORY NAZIANZEN

In fidelity to the example of the Master, it is vitally important for the Church today to go forth and preach the Gospel to all: to all places, on all occasions, without hesitation, reluctance, or fear. The joy of the Gospel is for all people: no one can be excluded.

—Apostolic Exhortation *The Joy of the Gospel*, 23

JANUARY 2

Saint Stephen

Today we pray especially for the Christians who are discriminated against on account of the witness they bear to Christ and to the Gospel. Let us remain close to these brothers and sisters who, like Saint Stephen, are unjustly accused and made the objects of various kinds of violence.

—Angelus Address, St. Peter's Square, December 26, 2013

DECEMBER 26

Most Holy Name of Jesus

What is God's love? It is not something vague, some generic feeling. God's love has a name and a face: Jesus Christ, Jesus.

—Angelus Address, St. Peter's Square, August 11, 2013

JANUARY 3

NATIVITY OF THE LORD

The birth of Jesus brings us the good news that we are loved immensely and uniquely by God, and he not only enables us to know this love, he also gives it to us; he communicates it to us!

—General Audience, St. Peter's Square, December 18, 2013

DECEMBER 25

Saint Elizabeth Ann Seton

In the Gospel the essential thing is *mercy*. . . . Jesus says this clearly, summarizing his teaching for the disciples: "Be merciful, even as your Father is merciful" (Luke 6:36). Can there be a Christian who isn't merciful? No. A Christian must necessarily be merciful, because this is the center of the Gospel.

—General Audience, St. Peter's Square, September 10, 2014

JANUARY 4

On this night, let us share the joy of the Gospel: God loves us, he so loves us that he gave us his Son to be our brother, to be light in our darkness. . . . Jesus is the light who brightens the darkness.

—Homily, St. Peter's Basilica, Midnight Mass, Solemnity of the Nativity of the Lord, December 24, 2013

DECEMBER 24

SAINT JOHN NEUMANN

Jesus is the Good Shepherd. He seeks us out and
he stays near us even though we are sinners,
indeed because we are sinners.

—Twitter, September 8, 2014

JANUARY 5

Saint John of Kanty

If God, in the Christmas mystery, reveals himself not as One who remains on high and dominates the universe but as the One who bends down, descends to the little and poor earth, it means that, to be like him, we should not put ourselves above others but indeed lower ourselves, place ourselves at the service of others.

—General Audience, St. Peter's Square, December 18, 2013

DECEMBER 23

The joy of the Gospel is not just any joy. It consists
in knowing one is welcomed and loved by God. . . .
Christian joy, like hope, is founded on God's fidelity,
on the certainty that he always keeps his promises.

—Angelus Address, St. Peter's Square, December 15, 2013

JANUARY 6

"This will be a sign for you: you will find a child wrapped in swaddling cloths and lying in a manger" (Luke 2:12).... The Child Jesus, born in Bethlehem, is the sign given by God to those who awaited salvation, and he remains forever the sign of God's tenderness and presence in our world.

—Homily, Bethlehem, Pilgrimage to the Holy Land, May 25, 2014

DECEMBER 22

Let us recognize that God is not something vague;
our God is not a God "spray"; he is tangible;
he is not abstract but has a name: "God is love."

—Angelus Address, St. Peter's Square,
Solemnity of the Most Holy Trinity, May 26, 2013

JANUARY 7

SAINT PETER CANISIUS

Jesus is never far from us sinners.
He wants to pour out on us, without limit,
all of his mercy.

—Twitter, March 24, 2014

DECEMBER 21

Our communion with the Lord obliges us, his disciples,
to imitate him, making our existence, through our behavior,
bread broken for others, as the Teacher has broken the
bread that is truly his flesh. . . . This means for us generous
conduct towards our neighbor, thereby demonstrating
the attitude of giving life for others.

—Angelus Address, St. Peter's Square,
Solemnity of the Most Holy Body and Blood of Christ, June 22, 2014

JANUARY 8

Let us make ourselves ready to celebrate Christmas by contemplating Mary and Joseph. . . . With them, let us walk together toward Bethlehem.

—Angelus Address, St. Peter's Square, December 22, 2013

DECEMBER 20

To live as true children of God means to love
our neighbor and to be close to those who
are lonely and in difficulty.

—Twitter, July 1, 2014

JANUARY 9

Mary is the Mother of God, our mother and mother of the Church. So many men and women, young and old, have turned to her to say "thank you" and to beg a favor. Mary takes us to Jesus and Jesus gives us peace. Let us turn to her, trusting in her assistance, with courage and hope.

—Address to Young People of the Dioceses
of Abruzzi and Molise, July 5, 2014

DECEMBER 19

We are called to love each other as Jesus loved us. And love is the concrete sign that demonstrates faith in God the Father, Son, and Holy Spirit. And love is the badge of the Christian, as Jesus told us: "By this all men will know that you are my disciples, if you have love for one another" (John 13:35).

—Angelus Address, St. Peter's Square,
Solemnity of the Most Holy Trinity, June 15, 2014

JANUARY 10

The Child of Bethlehem is frail. . . . Yet he is the Word made flesh who came to transform the hearts and lives of all men and women. This Child, like every other child, is vulnerable; he needs to be accepted and protected. Today too, children need to be welcomed and defended, from the moment of their conception.

—Homily, Bethlehem, Pilgrimage to the Holy Land, May 25, 2014

DECEMBER 18

Let us not forget this word: God never, ever tires of forgiving us! . . . The problem is that we ourselves tire; we do not want to ask; we grow weary of asking for forgiveness. He never tires of forgiving, but at times we get tired of asking for forgiveness.

—Angelus Address, St. Peter's Square, March 17, 2013

JANUARY 11

We are all simple but important instruments of [God];
we have not received the gift of faith to keep it hidden
but rather to spread it so that it can illumine a great
many of our brethren on their journey.

—Address to General Directors of Pontifical Missionary Works,
Clementine Hall, May 17, 2013

DECEMBER 17

All of us who are baptized are missionary disciples. We are called to become a living Gospel in the world.

—Twitter, February 25, 2014

JANUARY 12

True freedom is found in our loving embrace of the Father's will. From Mary, full of grace, we learn that Christian freedom is more than liberation from sin. . . . It is the freedom to love God and our brothers and sisters with a pure heart, and to live a life of joyful hope for the coming of Christ's kingdom.

—Homily, Apostolic Journey to the Republic of Korea,
August 15, 2014

DECEMBER 16

SAINT HILARY

Love of neighbor is a fundamental attitude that Jesus speaks of, and he says that our relationship with God cannot be honest if we are not willing to make peace with our neighbor.

—Angelus Address, St. Peter's Square, February 16, 2014

JANUARY 13

Far from divorcing us from reality, our faith in the Son of God
made man in Jesus of Nazareth enables us to grasp reality's
deepest meaning and to see how much God loves this world
and is constantly guiding it towards himself. This leads us,
as Christians, to live our lives in this world with ever-greater
commitment and intensity.

—Encyclical *The Light of Faith*, 18

DECEMBER 15

As when a mother takes her child upon her knee and caresses him or her: so the Lord will do and does with us. This is the cascade of tenderness which gives us much consolation. "As one whom his mother comforts, so I will comfort you" (Isaiah 66:13).

—Homily, St. Peter's Basilica, Mass with Seminarians, Novices, and Those Discerning Their Vocations, July 7, 2013

JANUARY 14

Saint John of the Cross

The cross of Christ reveals the power of God to bridge every division, to heal every wound, and to reestablish the original bonds of brotherly love. . . . Trust in the power of Christ's cross! Welcome its reconciling grace into your own hearts and share that grace with others!

—Homily at Mass for Peace and Reconciliation,
Seoul, August 18, 2014

DECEMBER 14

Prayer is the breath of faith: in a relationship of trust,
in a relationship of love, dialogue cannot be left out,
and prayer is the dialogue of the soul with God.

—Angelus Address, St. Peter's Square, October 6, 2013

JANUARY 15

SAINT LUCY

The Lord is always there waiting to give us his love: it is an amazing thing, one which never ceases to surprise us.

—Twitter, September 16, 2014

DECEMBER 13

The lifeblood of God's family, of the Church, is God's love, which is actualized in loving him and others, all others, without distinction or reservation. The Church is a family in which we love and are loved.

—General Audience, St. Peter's Square, May 29, 2013

JANUARY 16

Our Lady of Guadalupe

When the image of the Virgin appeared on the tilma of Juan Diego, it was the prophecy of an embrace: Mary's embrace of all the peoples of the vast expanses of America. . . . That is the message of Our Lady of Guadalupe. . . . I ask all the people of the Americas to open wide their arms, like the Virgin, with love and tenderness.

—General Audience, St. Peter's Square, December 11, 2013

DECEMBER 12

Saint Anthony of Egypt

There is so much noise in the world!
May we learn to be silent in our hearts and before God.

—Twitter, November 18, 2014

JANUARY 17

SAINT DAMASUS I

Let us ask for the help of Mary Most Holy so that the Church throughout the world may proclaim the resurrection of the Lord with candor and courage and give credible witness to it with signs of brotherly love. Brotherly love is the closest testimony we can give that Jesus is alive with us, that Jesus is risen.

—Regina Caeli Address, St. Peter's Square, April 14, 2013

DECEMBER 11

When we face daily life, when difficulties arise, let us remember this: "I can do all things in him who strengthens me" (Philippians 4:13). The Lord always strengthens us; he never lets strength lack. The Lord does not try us beyond our possibilities. He is always with us. "I can do all things in him who strengthens me."

—General Audience, St. Peter's Square, May 14, 2014

JANUARY 18

Jesus is God with us! Jesus is God with us always and forever with us in history's suffering and sorrow. The birth of Jesus reveals that God "sided" with man once and for all, to save us, to raise us from the dust of our misery, from our difficulty, from our sins.

—General Audience, St. Peter's Square, December 18, 2013

DECEMBER 10

Every injury, every one of our pains and sorrows, has been borne on the shoulders of the Good Shepherd who offered himself in sacrifice and thereby opened the way to eternal life. His open wounds are like the cleft through which the torrent of his mercy is poured out upon the world.

—Address on the 50th Anniversary of the Meeting between Pope Paul VI and Patriarch Athenagoras in Jerusalem, May 25, 2014

JANUARY 19

SAINT JUAN DIEGO

May the Virgin Mary help us to hasten our steps to Bethlehem, to encounter the Child who is born for us, for the salvation and joy of all people. . . . May she obtain for us the grace to live the joy of the Gospel in our families, at work, in the parish, and everywhere.

—Angelus Address, St. Peter's Square,
Third Sunday of Advent, December 15, 2013

DECEMBER 9

SAINT FABIAN; SAINT SEBASTIAN

As long as everyone seeks to accumulate for themselves,
there will be no justice. Instead, by entrusting ourselves
to God's providence, and seeking his kingdom together,
no one will lack the necessary means to live with dignity.

—Angelus Address, St. Peter's Square, March 2, 2014

JANUARY 20

Immaculate Conception of the Blessed Virgin Mary

By contemplating our beautiful Immaculate Mother,
let us also recognize our truest destiny, our deepest
vocation: to be loved, to be transformed by love,
to be transformed by the beauty of God.

—Angelus Address, St. Peter's Square, December 8, 2013

DECEMBER 8

Saint Agnes

For God, we are not numbers; we are important;
indeed we are the most important thing to him.
Even if we are sinners, we are what is closest to his heart.

—Homily, Basilica of St. John Lateran,
Divine Mercy Sunday, April 7, 2013

JANUARY 21

SAINT AMBROSE

All of us make mistakes in life and all of us, too, are sinners. And when we go to ask the Lord for forgiveness for our sins, for our mistakes, he always forgives us, he never tires of forgiving. He tells us, "Turn your back on this path; this is not the right one for you." And he helps us.

—Address at the Local Penitentiary of Isernia, July 5, 2014

DECEMBER 7

Every time a child is abandoned and an elderly person cast out, not only is it an act of injustice, but it also ensures the failure of that society. Caring for our little ones and for our elders is a choice for civilization.

—Address to the Plenary Assembly of the Pontifical Council for the Family, Clementine Hall, October 25, 2013

JANUARY 22

SAINT NICHOLAS

To pray for a person with whom I am irritated
is a beautiful step forward in love, and an act of
evangelization. Let us do it today! Let us not allow
ourselves to be robbed of the ideal of fraternal love!

—Apostolic Exhortation *The Joy of the Gospel*, 101

DECEMBER 6

SAINT VINCENT; SAINT MARIANNE COPE

No one is more patient than God the Father; no one
understands and knows how to wait as much as he does.

—Twitter, May 2, 2014

JANUARY 23

Mary sustains our journey toward Christmas, for she teaches us how to live this Advent Season in expectation of the Lord. For this time of Advent is a time of waiting for the Lord, who will visit us all on the feast, but also, each one, in our own hearts. The Lord is coming! Let us wait for him!

—Angelus Address, St. Peter's Square, December 8, 2013

DECEMBER 5

Saint Francis de Sales

[Christ's] Body . . . isn't simple nourishment to satisfy the body, like manna; the Body of Christ is the bread of the last times, capable of giving life, eternal life, because this bread is made of love.

—Homily, St. John Lateran Square,
Solemnity of the Most Holy Body and Blood of Christ, June 19, 2014

JANUARY 24

SAINT JOHN DAMASCENE

Compassion, sharing, Eucharist. This is the path that Jesus points out to us in this Gospel. A path which brings us to face the needs of this world with fraternity, but which leads us beyond this world, because it comes from God the Father and returns to him.

—Angelus Address, St. Peter's Square, August 3, 2014

DECEMBER 4

CONVERSION OF SAINT PAUL THE APOSTLE

"Who shall separate us from the love of Christ?" (Romans 8:35). With these words, Saint Paul speaks of the glory of our faith in Jesus: not only has Christ risen from the dead and ascended to heaven, but he has united us to himself and he grants us a share in his eternal life. Christ is victorious and his victory is ours!

—Homily at Mass for the Beatification of Korean Martyrs, Seoul, August 16, 2014

JANUARY 25

SAINT FRANCIS XAVIER

Jesus, help us to love God as Father
and our neighbor as ourselves.

—Twitter, June 30, 2014

DECEMBER 3

Saints Timothy and Titus

To have the Gospel in your hands, to have the Gospel on your bedside table, to have the Gospel in your pocket, to open it and read the word of Jesus: this is how the kingdom of God comes. Contact with the word of God draws us near to the kingdom of God.

—Homily, Park of the Royal Palace of Caserta, Italy, July 26, 2014

JANUARY 26

The more we unite ourselves to Jesus through prayer, Sacred Scripture, the Eucharist, the sacraments celebrated and lived in the Church and in fraternity, the more there will grow in us the joy of cooperating with God in the service of the kingdom of mercy and truth, of justice and peace.

—Message for the 51st World Day of Prayer for Vocations, May 11, 2014

DECEMBER 2

SAINT ANGELA MERICI

Jesus' friendship with us, his faithfulness and his mercy, are
a priceless gift which encourages us to follow him trustingly,
notwithstanding our failures, our mistakes, also our betrayals.

—Address, Church of Gethsemane,
Pilgrimage to the Holy Land, May 26, 2014

JANUARY 27

It is for the Christian to continually encounter Jesus, to watch him, to let himself be watched over by Jesus, because Jesus watches us with love; he loves us so much, he loves us so much, and he is always watching over us.

—Homily, Roman Parish of St. Cyril of Alexandria,
December 1, 2013

DECEMBER 1

SAINT THOMAS AQUINAS

The Christian who does not feel that the
Virgin Mary is his or her mother is an orphan.

—Twitter, September 2, 2014

JANUARY 28

SAINT ANDREW, APOSTLE

Dear brothers and sisters, the joy of finding the treasure of the kingdom of God shines through, it's visible. The Christian cannot keep his faith hidden, because it shines through in every word, in every deed, even the most simple and mundane: the love that God has given through Jesus shines through.

—Angelus Address, St. Peter's Square, July 27, 2014

NOVEMBER 30

We, by Baptism, are immersed in that inexhaustible source of life which is the death of Jesus, the greatest act of love in all of history; and thanks to this love we can live a new life, no longer at the mercy of evil, of sin and of death, but in communion with God and with our brothers and sisters.

—General Audience, St. Peter's Square, January 8, 2014

JANUARY 29

Jesus does not leave us on our own; he does not abandon his Church! He walks with us, he understands us. He understands our weaknesses, our sins; he forgives us always, if we let him forgive us. He is always with us, helping us to become less sinful, more holy, more united.

—General Audience, St. Pete's Square, August 27, 2014

NOVEMBER 29

We "believe" Jesus when we accept his word, his testimony, because he is truthful. We "believe in" Jesus when we personally welcome him into our lives and journey towards him, clinging to him in love and following in his footsteps along the way.

—Encyclical *The Light of Faith,* 18

JANUARY 30

Let us witness to the newness, hope, and joy that the Lord brings to life. Let us feel within us "the delightful and comforting joy of evangelizing" (*Evangelii Nuntiandi,* 80). Because evangelizing, proclaiming Jesus, gives us joy. Instead, egoism makes us bitter, sad, and depresses us. Evangelizing uplifts us.

—General Audience, St. Peter's Square, May 22, 2013

NOVEMBER 28

SAINT JOHN BOSCO

Wherever the Spirit of God reachcs,
everything is reborn and transfigured.

—Regina Caeli Address, St. Peter's Square, June 8, 2014

JANUARY 31

On our daily journey, especially in times of difficulty, in the battle against the evil that is outside and within us, the Lord is not far away; he is by our side. We battle with him beside us, and our weapon is prayer, which makes us feel his presence beside us, his mercy, and also his help.

—Angelus Address, St. Peter's Square, October 20, 2013

NOVEMBER 27

Jesus is our Advocate: how beautiful it is to hear this! . . . Let us not be afraid to turn to him to ask forgiveness, to ask for a blessing, to ask for mercy! He always pardons us; he is our Advocate: he always defends us! Don't forget this!

—General Audience, St. Peter's Square, April 17, 2013

FEBRUARY 1

The family which experiences the joy of faith communicates it naturally. That family is the salt of the earth and the light of the world; it is the leaven of society as a whole. Dear families, always live in faith and simplicity, like the Holy Family of Nazareth!

—Homily, St. Peter's Square, Family Day on the Occasion of the Year of Faith, October 27, 2013

NOVEMBER 26

PRESENTATION OF THE LORD

Simeon and Anna, upon seeing the child, knew immediately that he was the one long awaited by the people. They gave prophetic expression to the joy of encountering the Redeemer and, in a certain sense, served as a preparation for the encounter between the Messiah and the people.

—Homily, International Stadium,
Amman, Jordan, May 24, 2014

FEBRUARY 2

SAINT CATHERINE OF ALEXANDRIA

The Christian is a person who thinks and acts in accordance with God. . . . Do we think in accordance with God? Do we act in accordance with God? Or do we let ourselves be guided by the many other things that certainly do not come from God? Each one of us needs to respond to this in the depths of his or her own heart.

—General Audience, St. Peter's Square, May 8, 2013

NOVEMBER 25

Saint Blaise; Saint Ansgar

When we go to Confession, the Lord tells us: "I forgive you. But now come with me." And he helps us to get back on the path. He never condemns. He never simply forgives, but he forgives and accompanies. . . . He always takes us by the hand again. This is the love of God, and we must imitate it!

—Address, Pastoral Visit to the Penitentiary in Cosenza, June 21, 2014

FEBRUARY 3

SAINT ANDREW DUNG-LAC AND COMPANIONS

So often we today can find our faith challenged by the world, and in countless ways we are asked to compromise our faith, to water down the radical demands of the Gospel, and to conform to the spirit of this age. Yet the martyrs . . . challenge us to think about what, if anything, we ourselves would be willing to die for.

—Homily at Mass for the Beatification of Korean Martyrs,
Seoul, August 16, 2014

NOVEMBER 24

At the moment of temptation . . . there is no arguing with
Satan, our defense must always be the word of God!
And this will save us. In his replies to Satan, the Lord, using the
word of God, reminds us above all that "man shall not live by
bread alone, but by every word that proceeds
from the mouth of God" (Matthew 4:4).

—Angelus Address, St. Peter's Square,
First Sunday of Lent, March 9, 2014

FEBRUARY 4

SAINT CLEMENT I; SAINT COLUMBAN; BLESSED MIGUEL PRO

To live by faith means to put our lives in the hands of God, especially in our most difficult moments.

—Twitter, May 23, 2014

NOVEMBER 23

SAINT AGATHA

Our mission as Christians is to conform ourselves
evermore to Jesus as the model of our lives.

—Twitter, May 16, 2014

FEBRUARY 5

SAINT CECILIA

We cannot become starched Christians, those over-educated Christians who speak of theological matters as they calmly sip their tea. No! We must become courageous Christians and go in search of the people who are the very flesh of Christ, those who [need help most]!

—Address, St. Peter's Square, Vigil of Pentecost with Ecclesial Movements, May 18, 2013

NOVEMBER 22

SAINT PAUL MIKI AND COMPANIONS

The martyrs call out to us to put Christ first and to see all else in this world in relation to him and his eternal kingdom.

—Homily at Mass for the Beatification of Korean Martyrs,
Seoul, August 16, 2014

FEBRUARY 6

Presentation of the Blessed Virgin Mary

Mary lived perpetually immersed in the mystery of God-made-man, as his first and perfect disciple, by contemplating all things in her heart in the light of the Holy Spirit, in order to understand and live out the will of God.

—General Audience, St. Peter's Square, October 23, 2013

NOVEMBER 21

Who robs you of hope? The spirit of the world, wealth, the spirit of vanity, arrogance, pride. All these things steal hope from you. Where do I find hope? In the poor Jesus, Jesus who made himself poor for us. . . . Poverty demands that we sow hope. It requires me to have greater hope too.

—Dialogue with Students of Jesuit Schools of Italy and Albania, Paul VI Audience Hall, June 7, 2013

FEBRUARY 7

The Holy Spirit draws us into the mystery of the living God and saves us from the threat of a Church which is gnostic and self-referential, closed in on herself; he impels us to open the doors and go forth to proclaim and bear witness to the good news of the Gospel, to communicate the joy of faith, the encounter with Christ.

—Homily, St. Peter's Square,
Solemnity of Pentecost, May 19, 2013

NOVEMBER 20

SAINT JEROME EMILIANI; SAINT JOSEPHINE BAKHITA

To hear and accept God's call, to make a home for Jesus, you must be able to rest in the Lord. You must make time each day to rest in the Lord, to pray. To pray is to rest in the Lord.

—Meeting with Families, Mall of Asia Arena, Manila, January 16, 2015

FEBRUARY 8

Commit yourselves to great ideals, to the most important things. We Christians were not chosen by the Lord for little things; push onwards toward the highest principles. Stake your lives on noble ideals.

—Homily, St. Peter's Square, Mass and Conferral of the Sacrament of Confirmation, April 28, 2013

NOVEMBER 19

Like the Good Samaritan, may we not be ashamed
of touching the wounds of those who suffer,
but try to heal them with concrete acts of love.

—Twitter, June 5, 2014

FEBRUARY 9

DEDICATION OF THE BASILICAS OF SAINTS PETER AND PAUL IN ROME; SAINT ROSE PHILIPPINE DUCHESNE

We all have to proclaim and bear witness to the Gospel. We should all ask ourselves: How do I bear witness to Christ through my faith? Do I have the courage of Peter and the other apostles, to think, to choose, and to live as a Christian, obedient to God?

—Homily, Basilica of St. Paul Outside-the-Walls, April 14, 2013

NOVEMBER 18

SAINT SCHOLASTICA

What is the measure of God? Without measure! The measure of God is without measure. Everything! Everything! Everything! It's impossible to measure the love of God: it is without measure!

—Angelus Address, St. Peter's Square,
Solemnity of the Most Holy Body and Blood of Christ, June 22, 2014

FEBRUARY 10

SAINT ELIZABETH OF HUNGARY

In Christ we contemplate God's faithfulness. Every act, every word of Jesus reveals the merciful and steadfast love of the Father. . . . Above all, we can say to the Lord, "Lord Jesus, render my heart ever more like yours, full of love and faithfulness."

—Homily, Gemelli Hospital,
Solemnity of the Most Sacred Heart of Jesus, June 27, 2014

NOVEMBER 17

Our Lady of Lourdes

Let us invoke the Virgin Mary as Mother of Divine Providence.
To her we entrust our lives, the journey of the Church and all
humanity. In particular, let us invoke her intercession that we
may all strive to live in a simple and sober manner, keeping in
mind the needs of those brothers who are most in need.

—Angelus Address, St. Peter's Square, March 2, 2014

FEBRUARY 11

When a man and woman celebrate the Sacrament of Matrimony, God as it were "is mirrored" in them; he impresses in them his own features and the indelible character of his love. Marriage is the icon of God's love for us.

—General Audience, St. Peter's Square, April 2, 2014

NOVEMBER 16

This, our faith in the true presence of Jesus Christ, true God and true Man, in the consecrated bread and wine, is authentic if we commit ourselves to *walk behind him and with him*. . . . People who adore God in the Eucharist are people who walk in charity.

—Homily, Pastoral Visit to Cassano all'Jonio,
Calabria, June 21, 2014

FEBRUARY 12

SAINT ALBERT THE GREAT

Come, Holy Spirit! Help us to overcome our selfishness.

—Twitter, May 20, 2014

NOVEMBER 15

God is joyful! . . . The joy of God is forgiving! The joy of a shepherd who finds his little lamb; the joy of a woman who finds her coin; it is the joy of a father welcoming home the son who was lost, who was as though dead and has come back to life, who has come home.

—Angelus Address, St. Peter's Square, September 15, 2013

FEBRUARY 13

What is important is not to stand still. We all know that when water stands still it stagnates. There's a saying in Spanish that says, "Standing water is the first to go bad." Do not stand still. We all have to walk, to take a step every day, with the Lord's help. God is Father, he is mercy, he always loves us.

—Address at the Local Penitentiary of Isernia, July 5, 2014

NOVEMBER 14

SAINTS CYRIL AND METHODIUS

May we never talk about others behind their backs,
but speak to them openly about what we think.

—Twitter, June 9, 2014

FEBRUARY 14

SAINT FRANCES XAVIER CABRINI

Being Christian is not just obeying orders but means being in Christ, thinking like him, acting like him, loving like him; it means letting him take possession of our life and change it, transform it, and free it from the darkness of evil and sin.

—General Audience, St. Peter's Square, April 10, 2013

NOVEMBER 13

The message which Christians bring to the world is this: Jesus, Love incarnate, died on the cross for our sins, but God the Father raised him and made him the Lord of life and death. In Jesus love has triumphed over hatred, mercy over sinfulness, goodness over evil, truth over falsehood, life over death.

—*Urbi et Orbi* Message, Easter Sunday, April 20, 2014

FEBRUARY 15

SAINT JOSAPHAT

We need to rediscover a contemplative spirit
so that the love of God may warm our hearts.

—Twitter, April 8, 2014

NOVEMBER 12

Let us not forget that the Lord always watches over us with mercy; he always watches over us with mercy. Let us not be afraid of approaching him! He has a merciful heart! If we show him our inner wounds, our inner sins, he will always forgive us. It is pure mercy. Let us go to Jesus!

—Angelus Address, St. Peter's Square, June 9, 2013

FEBRUARY 16

Jesus gave himself up to death on the cross, to free us from the power of darkness and to move us to the kingdom of life, of beauty, of goodness, and of joy. To read the Gospel is to find Jesus and to have this Christian joy, which is a gift of the Holy Spirit.

—Angelus Address, St. Peter's Square, July 27, 2014

NOVEMBER 11

SEVEN HOLY FOUNDERS OF THE SERVITE ORDER

May we enter into true friendship with Jesus
so that following him closely, we may live with and for him.

—Twitter, May 29, 2014

FEBRUARY 17

SAINT LEO THE GREAT

Jesus asks us to believe that forgiveness is the door
which leads to reconciliation. In telling us to forgive our
brothers unreservedly, he is asking us to do something utterly
radical, but he also gives us the grace to do it.

—Homily at Mass for Peace and Reconciliation,
Seoul, August 18, 2014

NOVEMBER 10

Faith is born of an encounter with the living God who calls us
and reveals his love, a love which precedes us and upon which
we can lean for security and for building our lives. . . . Faith,
received from God as a supernatural gift, becomes a light for
our way, guiding our journey through time.

—Encyclical *The Light of Faith,* 4

FEBRUARY 18

DEDICATION OF THE BASILICA OF SAINT JOHN LATERAN IN ROME

God's love is unbounded: it has no limits!

—Twitter, August 26, 2014

NOVEMBER 9

In our day, Jesus' command to "go and make disciples" echoes in the changing scenarios and ever new challenges to the Church's mission of evangelization, and all of us . . . are asked to obey his call to go forth from our own comfort zone in order to reach all the "peripheries" in need of the light of the Gospel.

—Apostolic Exhortation *The Joy of the Gospel,* 20

FEBRUARY 19

Christians are "spiritual." This does not mean that we are people who live "in the clouds," far removed from real life, as if it were some kind of mirage. . . . Those who let themselves be led by the Holy Spirit are realists; they know how to survey and assess reality.

—Homily, St. Peter's Square,
Mass for *Evangelium Vitae* Day, June 16, 2013

NOVEMBER 8

Truth is not found in a laboratory; it is found in life, seeking Jesus in order to find it. But the greatest, most beautiful mystery is that when we find Jesus, we realize that he was seeking us first, that he found us first, because he came before us! . . . He precedes us and always awaits us. He is before us.

—Address at Meeting with Evangelical Pastor,
Caserta, Italy, July 28, 2014

FEBRUARY 20

The Eucharist is at the heart of "Christian initiation," together with Baptism and Confirmation, and it constitutes the source of the Church's life itself. From this sacrament of love, in fact, flows every authentic journey of faith, of communion, and of witness.

—General Audience, St. Peter's Square, February 5, 2014

NOVEMBER 7

SAINT PETER DAMIAN

When we hear the word of Jesus, when we listen to the word of Jesus and carry it in our heart, this word grows. Do you know how it grows? By giving it to the other! The word of Christ grows in us when we proclaim it, when we give it to others! And this is what Christian life is. . . . Listen to Jesus and offer him to others.

—Angelus Address, St. Peter's Square, March 16, 2014

FEBRUARY 21

The joy of the Gospel is such that it cannot be taken away from us by anyone or anything (cf. John 16:22). . . . With the eyes of faith, we can see the light which the Holy Spirit always radiates in the midst of darkness, never forgetting that "where sin increased, grace has abounded all the more" (Romans 5:20).

—Apostolic Exhortation *The Joy of the Gospel,* 84

NOVEMBER 6

CHAIR OF SAINT PETER THE APOSTLE

How much do I love the Church? . . . What do I do to ensure
that she is a community in which each one feels welcomed and
understood, feels the mercy and love of God who renews life?
Faith is a gift and an act which concern us personally, but God
calls us to live with our faith together, as a family, as Church.

—General Audience, St. Peter's Square, May 29, 2013

FEBRUARY 22

Our sins are in the hands of God; those merciful hands, those hands "wounded" by love. It was not by chance that Jesus willed to preserve the wounds in his hands to enable us to know and feel his mercy. And this is our strength, our hope.

—Homily, St. Peter's Basilica, November 4, 2013

NOVEMBER 5

We will never be disillusioned or
lose our way if we are guided by God.

—Twitter, May 22, 2014

FEBRUARY 23

SAINT CHARLES BORROMEO

Dear brothers and sisters, we need to let ourselves be
bathed in the light of the Holy Spirit so that he may lead
us into the Truth of God, who is the one Lord of our life.

—General Audience, St. Peter's Square, May 15, 2013

NOVEMBER 4

God's becoming man is a great mystery! But the reason
for all this is his love, a love which is grace, generosity,
a desire to draw near, a love which does not hesitate to
offer itself in sacrifice for the beloved.

—Message for Lent 2014

FEBRUARY 24

Saint Martin de Porres

Let us open ourselves to the light of the Lord;
he awaits us always in order to enable us to see better,
to give us more light, to forgive us. Let us not forget this!

—Angelus Address, St. Peter's Square, March 30, 2014

NOVEM

Blessed are those who have not seen but have believed: this is the beatitude of faith! In every epoch and in every place, blessed are those who, on the strength of the word of God proclaimed in the Church and witnessed by Christians, believe that Jesus Christ is the love of God incarnate, Mercy incarnate.

—Regina Caeli Address, St. Peter's Square, April 7, 2013

FEBRUARY 25

ALL SOULS

All baptized persons here on earth, the souls in purgatory, and all the blessed who are already in paradise make one great family. This communion between earth and heaven is realized especially in intercessory prayer.

—General Audience, St. Peter's Square, October 30, 2013

NOVEMBER 2

What does "People of God" mean? First of all, it means that God does not belong in a special way to any one people, for it is he who calls us, convokes us, invites us to be part of his people, and this invitation is addressed to all, without distinction, for the mercy of God "desires all men to be saved" (1 Timothy 2:4).

—General Audience, St. Peter's Square, June 12, 2013

FEBRUARY 26

ALL SAINTS

The saints give us a message. They tell us: trust in the Lord
because the Lord does not disappoint! He never disappoints;
he is a good friend always at our side.

—Angelus Address, St. Peter's Square,
Solemnity of All Saints, November 1, 2013

NOVEMBER 1

We are not Christians on an individual basis, each one on his or her own; no, our Christian identity is to belong! We are Christians because we belong to the Church. It is like a last name: if the first name is "I am Christian," the last name is "I belong to the Church."

—General Audience, St. Peter's Square, June 25, 2014

FEBRUARY 27

Jesus' resurrection does not only give us the certainty of life after death, it also illumines the very mystery of the death of each one of us. If we live united to Jesus, faithful to him, we will also be able to face the passage of death with hope and serenity.

—General Audience, St. Peter's Square, November 27, 2013

OCTOBER 31

How much prayer a bishop, a cardinal, a pope needs in order to help and lead forward the people of God! . . . The vocation of the bishop, cardinal, and pope is precisely this: to be a servant, to serve in the name of Christ. Pray for us, that we might be good servants: good servants, not good masters!

—Angelus Address, St. Peter's Square, February 23, 2014

FEBRUARY 28

The Lord never disappoints. Feel in your heart if the Lord
is calling you to follow him. Let's let his gaze rest on us,
hear his voice, and follow him!

—Angelus Address, St. Peter's Square, January 26, 2014

OCTOBER 30

God isn't far and insensitive to our human affairs. He is close to us, always beside us, walking with us to share our joys and our sorrows, our hopes and our struggles. He loves us very much, and for that reason he became man; he came into the world not to condemn it, but so the world would be saved through Jesus (cf. John 3:16-17).

—Angelus Address, St. Peter's Square,
Solemnity of the Most Holy Trinity, June 15, 2014

FEBRUARY 29

Man is like a traveler who, crossing the deserts of life, thirsts for the living water: gushing and fresh, capable of quenching his deep desire for light, love, beauty, and peace. We all feel this desire! And Jesus gives us this living water: he is the Holy Spirit, who proceeds from the Father and whom Jesus pours out into our hearts.

—General Audience, St. Peter's Square, May 8, 2013

OCTOBER 29

Consider this: a small Gospel always at hand,
ready to open when the opportunity arises,
ready to read what Jesus says. Jesus is there.

—Homily, Park of the Royal Palace of
Caserta, Italy, July 26, 2014

MARCH 1

SAINTS SIMON AND JUDE, APOSTLES

Every vocation, even within the variety of paths,
always requires an exodus from oneself in order
to center one's life on Christ and on his Gospel.

—Message for the 51ˢᵗ World Day of Prayer for Vocations,
May 11, 2014

OCTOBER 28

[Jesus] understands human sufferings; he has shown the face of God's mercy, and he has bent down to heal body and soul. . . . This is his heart which looks to all of us, to our sicknesses, to our sins. The love of Jesus is great.

—Homily, St. Peter's Square,
Palm Sunday, March 24, 2013

MARCH 2

God shows us that he is the good Father. And how does he do this? . . . He does it through the incarnation of his Son, who becomes one of us. Through this actual man called Jesus, we are able to understand what God truly intends. He wants free human beings so they always feel protected as children of a good Father.

—Homily at Celebration of Vespers with Young German Altar Servers, St. Peter's Square, August 5, 2014

OCTOBER 27

Saint Katharine Drexel

Let us learn from Christ how to pray, to forgive,
to sow peace, and to be near those in need.

—Twitter, February 19, 2014

MARCH 3

To evangelize . . . it is necessary to open ourselves once again to the horizon of God's Spirit, without being afraid of what he asks us or of where he leads us. Let us entrust ourselves to him! He will enable us to live out and bear witness to our faith, and will illuminate the heart of those we meet.

—General Audience, St. Peter's Square, May 22, 2013

OCTOBER 26

During the season of Lent, the Church issues two important invitations: to have a greater awareness of the redemptive work of Christ; and to live out one's Baptism with deeper commitment.

—General Audience, St. Peter's Square,
Ash Wednesday, March 5, 2014

MARCH 4

What is the most important reality for you, the most precious reality, the one that attracts your heart like a magnet? . . . May I say that it is God's love? Do you wish to do good to others, to live for the Lord and for your brothers and sisters? May I say this? Each one answer in his own heart.

—Angelus Address, St. Peter's Square, August 11, 2013

OCTOBER 25

Faith is first of all a gift we have received. But in order to bear fruit, God's grace always demands our openness to him, our free and tangible response.

—General Audience, St. Peter's Square, April 24, 2013

MARCH 5

SAINT ANTHONY MARY CLARET

Saint Paul reminds us, "If we are faithless, he, Jesus, remains faithful for he cannot deny himself" (cf. 2 Timothy 2:13). Jesus remains faithful, he never betrays us: even when we were wrong, he always waits for us to forgive us. He is the face of the merciful Father.

—Homily, Gemelli Hospital,
Solemnity of the Most Sacred Heart of Jesus, June 27, 2014

OCTOBER 24

For us Christians, wherever the cross is, there is hope, always. . . . That is why I like to say: do not allow yourselves to be robbed of hope. May we not be robbed of hope, because this strength is a grace, a gift from God which carries us forward with our eyes fixed on heaven.

—Homily, Castel Gandolfo, August 15, 2013

MARCH 6

SAINT JOHN OF CAPISTRANO

Creation is a gift; it is the marvelous gift that God has given us
so that we will take care of it and harness it for the benefit of all,
always with great respect and gratitude.

—General Audience, St. Peter's Square, May 21, 2014

OCTOBER 23

SAINTS PERPETUA AND FELICITY

Lent is a time of grace, a time to convert
and live out our Baptism fully.

—Twitter, March 27, 2014

MARCH 7

SAINT JOHN PAUL II

To be conquered by the love of God! This is a beautiful thing.
To allow ourselves to be conquered by this love of a father,
who loves us so, loves us with all his heart.

—General Audience, St. Peter's Square, June 11, 2014

OCTOBER 22

Saint John of God

Today, as the Church seeks to experience a profound missionary renewal, there is a kind of preaching which falls to each of us as a daily responsibility. It has to do with bringing the Gospel to the people we meet, whether they be our neighbors or complete strangers.

—Apostolic Exhortation *The Joy of the Gospel,* 127

MARCH 8

Even today Jesus asks his disciples—that is, all of us: "Who do you say that I am?" What do we answer? Let us think about this. But above all, let us pray to God . . . that he grant us the grace to respond, with a sincere heart: "You are the Christ, the Son of the living God." This is a confession of faith, this is really "the Creed."

—Angelus Address, St. Peter's Square, August 24, 2014

OCTOBER 21

SAINT FRANCES OF ROME

God does not wait for us to go to him, but it is
he who moves toward us, without calculation,
without quantification. That is what God is like.
He always takes the first step; he comes toward us.

—General Audience, St. Peter's Square, March 27, 2013

MARCH 9

Saint Paul of the Cross

The proof of authentic faith in Christ is self-giving and the spreading of love for our neighbors, especially for those who do not merit it, for the suffering and for the marginalized.

—Message for the 22nd World Day of the Sick 2014

OCTOBER 20

Lent is a fitting time for self-denial; we would do well to ask ourselves what we can give up in order to help and enrich others by our own poverty. Let us not forget that real poverty hurts: no self-denial is real without this dimension of penance. I distrust a charity that costs nothing and does not hurt.

—Message for Lent 2014

MARCH 10

SAINTS ISAAC JOGUES AND JOHN DE BRÉBEUF AND COMPANIONS

Faith can only be communicated through witness, and that
means love. Not with our own ideas but with the Gospel,
lived out in our own lives and brought to life within us
by the Holy Spirit. . . . Witness is what counts!

—Address, St. Peter's Square, Vigil of Pentecost
with Ecclesial Movements, May 18, 2013

OCTOBER 19

Faith does not merely gaze at Jesus, but sees
things as Jesus himself sees them, with his own eyes:
it is a participation in his way of seeing.

—Encyclical *The Light of Faith*, 18

MARCH 11

SAINT LUKE, EVANGELIST

Read the Gospel. Read the Gospel. . . . To read a passage of
the Gospel every day; and to carry a little Gospel with us—in
our pocket, in a purse—in some way to keep it at hand. And
there, reading a passage, we will find Jesus. Everything takes on
meaning when you find your treasure there, in the Gospel.

—Angelus Address, St. Peter's Square, July 27, 2014

OCTOBER 18

The battle against evil is a long and hard one; it requires patience and endurance, like Moses who had to keep his arms outstretched for the people to prevail (cf. Exodus 17:8-13). This is how it is: there is a battle to be waged each day, but God is our ally; faith in him is our strength and prayer is the expression of this faith.

—Angelus Address, St. Peter's Square, October 20, 2013

MARCH 12

Saint Ignatius of Antioch

The primary reason for evangelizing is the love of Jesus which we have received, the experience of salvation which urges us to ever greater love of him. What kind of love would not feel the need to speak of the beloved, to point him out, to make him known?

—Apostolic Exhortation *The Joy of the Gospel*, 264

OCTOBER 17

If one accumulates only for oneself, what will happen when one is called by God? No one can take his riches with him, because—as you know—the shroud has no pockets! It is better to share, for we can take with us to heaven only what we have shared with others.

—Angelus Address, St. Peter's Square, March 2, 2014

MARCH 13

When one lives attached to money, pride,
or power, it is impossible to be truly happy.

—Twitter, July 24, 2014

OCTOBER 16

What a beautiful truth of faith this is for our lives: the mercy of God! God's love for us is so great, so deep; it is an unfailing love, one which always takes us by the hand and supports us, lifts us up, and leads us on.

—Homily, Basilica of St. John Lateran, Divine Mercy Sunday, April 7, 2013

MARCH 14

SAINT TERESA OF ÁVILA

Our words can do much good and also much harm; they can heal and they can wound; they can encourage and they can dishearten. Remember: what counts is not what goes in but what comes out of the mouth and of the heart.

—Angelus Address, St. Peter's Square, July 13, 2014

OCTOBER 15

Jesus gave himself up to death voluntarily in order to reciprocate the love of God the Father, in perfect union with his will, to demonstrate his love for us. On the cross Jesus "loved me and gave himself for me" (Galatians 2:20). Each one of us can say: "He loved me and gave himself for me." Each one can say this "for me."

—General Audience, St. Peter's Square, March 27, 2013

MARCH 15

SAINT CALLISTUS I

Every encounter with Jesus changes our lives, always. It is a step forward, a step closer to God. And thus every encounter with Jesus changes our life. It is always, always this way.

—Angelus Address, St. Peter's Square, March 23, 2014

OCTOBER 14

There are no difficulties, trials, or misunderstandings to fear, provided we remain united to God as branches to the vine, provided we do not lose our friendship with him, provided we make ever more room for him in our lives. . . . God grants strength to our weakness, riches to our poverty, conversion and forgiveness to our sinfulness.

—Homily, St. Peter's Square, Mass and Conferral of the Sacrament of Confirmation, April 28, 2013

MARCH 16

God has a memory; he is not forgetful. God does not forget us, he always remembers. There is a passage in the Bible which says, "Even should a mother forget her child"—which is impossible— "I will never forget you" (cf. Isaiah 49:15). And this is true: God thinks about me, God remembers me. I am in God's memory.

—Address at the Local Penitentiary of Isernia, July 5, 2014

OCTOBER 13

Saint Patrick

It will do us good to take the crucifix in hand and kiss it many, many times and say: thank you Jesus, thank you Lord.

—General Audience, St. Peter's Square,
Wednesday in Holy Week, April 16, 2014

MARCH 17

It's not enough to love those who love us. Jesus says that pagans do this. It's not enough to do good to those who do good to us. To change the world for the better it is necessary to do good to those who are not able to return the favor, as the Father has done with us, by giving us Jesus. . . . Do good and carry on!

—General Audience, St. Peter's Square, September 10, 2014

OCTOBER 12

SAINT CYRIL OF JERUSALEM

Lent is a "powerful" season, a turning point that can
foster change and conversion in each of us. We all need to
improve, to change for the better. Lent helps us, and thus
we leave behind old habits and the lazy addiction to
the evil that deceives and ensnares us.

—General Audience, St. Peter's Square,
Ash Wednesday, March 5, 2014

MARCH 18

You may be like the son who left home, who sank to the depths, farthest from the Gospel. When you have the strength to say, "I want to come home," you will find the door open. God will come to meet you because he is always waiting for you.

—General Audience, St. Peter's Square, October 2, 2013

OCTOBER 11

Saint Joseph, Spouse of the Blessed Virgin Mary

Let us fervently call upon Mary Most Holy, the Mother of Jesus and our Mother, and Saint Joseph, her spouse. Let us ask them to enlighten, comfort, and guide every family in the world so that they may fulfill with dignity and peace the mission which God has entrusted to them.

—Angelus Address, St. Peter's Square,
Feast of the Holy Family of Nazareth, December 29, 2013

MARCH 19

Every day we must let Christ transform us and conform us to him. . . . The temptation to set God aside in order to put ourselves at the center is always at the door, and the experience of sin injures our Christian life, our being children of God.

—General Audience, St. Peter's Square, April 10, 2013

OCTOBER 10

Authentic faith, conversion, and openness of heart
to the brethren: these are the essential elements
for living the season of Lent.

—General Audience, St. Peter's Square,
Ash Wednesday, March 5, 2014

MARCH 20

When you are sad, take up the word of God. When you are down, take up the word of God and go to Sunday Mass and receive Communion, to participate in the mystery of Jesus. The word of God, the Eucharist: they fill us with joy.

—Regina Caeli Address, St. Peter's Square, May 4, 2014

OCTOBER 9

The Lord looks at us. He looks at us first. . . . I feel great comfort when I think of the Lord looking at me. We think we have to pray and talk, talk, talk. . . . No! Let the Lord look at you. When he looks at us, he gives us strength and helps us to bear witness to him.

—Address, St. Peter's Square, Vigil of Pentecost
with Ecclesial Movements, May 18, 2013

MARCH 21

Let us ask ourselves today: are we open to "God's surprises"?
Or are we closed and fearful before the newness of the Holy
Spirit? Do we have the courage to strike out along the new paths
which God's newness sets before us, or do we resist, barricaded
in transient structures which have lost their capacity for
openness to what is new?

—Homily, St. Peter's Square,
Solemnity of Pentecost, May 19, 2013

OCTOBER 8

It has been said that the only real regret lies in not being a saint; we could also say that there is only one real kind of poverty: not living as children of God and brothers and sisters of Christ.

—Message for Lent 2014

MARCH 22

OUR LADY OF THE ROSARY

The Rosary is a school of prayer; the Rosary is a school of faith!

—Angelus Address, St. Peter's Square, October 6, 2013

OCTOBER 7

SAINT TURIBIUS OF MOGROVEJO

Jesus' word is the most nourishing food for the soul: it nourishes our souls, it nourishes our faith! I suggest that each day you take a few minutes and read a nice passage of the Gospel and hear what happens there. Hearing Jesus, and each day Jesus' word enters our hearts and makes us stronger in faith.

—Homily, Roman Parish of Santa Maria dell' Orazione,
March 16, 2014

MARCH 23

Saint Bruno; Blessed Marie-Rose Durocher

You know, words too can kill! When I speak, when I make an unfair criticism, when I "flay" a brother with my tongue, this is killing another person's reputation! Words kill too. Let us pay attention to this.

—Angelus Address, St. Peter's Square, September 7, 2014

OCTOBER 6

Are we often weary, disheartened, and sad? Do we feel weighed down by our sins? Do we think that we won't be able to cope? Let us not close our hearts; let us not lose confidence; let us never give up. There are no situations which God cannot change; there is no sin which he cannot forgive if only we open ourselves to him.

—Homily, St. Peter's Basilica,
Easter Vigil, March 30, 2013

MARCH 24

Let us ask the Holy Spirit for the grace to live daily
according to the mind of Jesus and his Gospel.

—Twitter, May 15, 2014

OCTOBER 5

ANNUNCIATION OF THE LORD

The Virgin Mary teaches us what it means to live in the Holy Spirit and what it means to accept the news of God in our life. She conceived Jesus by the work of the Holy Spirit, and every Christian, each one of us, is called to accept the Word of God, to accept Jesus inside of us, and then to bring him to everyone.

—Regina Caeli Address, St. Peter's Square, April 28, 2013

MARCH 25

SAINT FRANCIS OF ASSISI

Let us all remember this: one cannot proclaim the Gospel of Jesus without the tangible witness of one's life. . . . I am thinking now of some advice that Saint Francis of Assisi gave his brothers: preach the Gospel and, if necessary, use words. Preaching with your life, with your witness.

—Homily, Basilica of St. Paul Outside-the-Walls, April 14, 2013

OCTOBER 4

[Jesus] stooped down to us and by his love he restored our dignity and brought us salvation. Jesus' humility never fails to move us, the fact that he bends down to wounded humanity in order to heal us: he bends down to heal all our wounds!

—Address to Refugees and Disabled Young People, Latin Church, Bethany beyond the Jordan, May 24, 2014

MARCH 26

Be missionaries of God's love and tenderness!
Be missionaries of God's mercy, which always forgives us,
always awaits us, and loves us dearly.

—Homily, St. Peter's Square, May 5, 2013

OCTOBER 3

Because Jesus rose, we will rise; we have the hope of resurrection because he has opened to us the door of resurrection. And this transformation, this transfiguration of our bodies, is prepared for in this life by our relationship with Jesus in the sacraments, especially in the Eucharist.

—General Audience, St. Peter's Square, December 4, 2013

MARCH 27

HOLY GUARDIAN ANGELS

In the trials of life, we are not alone; we are accompanied and sustained by the angels of God, who offer, so to speak, their wings to help us overcome the many dangers, to be able to fly above those realities that can make our lives difficult or drag us down.

—Blessing of Statue of St. Michael the Archangel,
Vatican Gardens, July 5, 2013

OCTOBER 2

We must protect creation for it is a gift which the Lord has given us. It is God's present to us; we are the guardians of creation. When we exploit creation, we destroy that sign of God's love. To destroy creation is to say to God, "I don't care." And this is not good: this is sin.

—General Audience, St. Peter's Square, May 21, 2014

MARCH 28

SAINT THÉRÈSE OF LISIEUX

Contrition is the way to repentance, that favored path that
leads to the heart of God, which embraces us and gives
us another chance, which always opens us to the truth of
atonement and by his mercy allows us to transform.

—Letter to the 19th International Congress of the
International Association of Penal Law, May 30, 2014

OCTOBER 1

The Word Among Us Press
Daily Stand-Up Calendars

Our popular stand-up calendars will inspire you each day with quotes from Catholic saints, spiritual writers, and Scripture. Order one for your kitchen counter, your bedside table, and your desk—they can be used year after year! These Catholic calendars also make wonderful gifts for friends and family.

To order, call our customer service line at 1-800-775-9673.

Order online at waubooks.org and save 10%.

Stand-Up Calendars from The Word Among Us

No Bible, No Breakfast
No Bible, No Bed

Wisdom from
Women Saints

Pope John Paul II:
Words to Live By

Day by Day with Mary,
the Mother of God

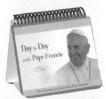

Day by Day
with Pope Francis

Journey with
the Saints

To order, call our customer service line at 1-800-775-9673.

Order online at waubooks.org and save 10%.

God does not forget us, the Father never abandons us. He is a patient father, always waiting for us! He respects our freedom, but he remains faithful forever. And when we come back to him, he welcomes us like children into his house, for he never ceases, not for one instant, to wait for us with love.

—Angelus Address, St. Peter's Square, September 15, 2013

MARCH 29

This is important: the courage to trust in Jesus' mercy, to trust in his patience, to seek refuge always in the wounds of his love.

—Homily, Basilica of St. John Lateran,
Divine Mercy Sunday, April 7, 2013

SEPTEMBER 30

The Holy Spirit constitutes the soul, the lifeblood of the Church, and of every individual Christian: He is the Love of God who makes of our hearts his dwelling place and enters into communion with us. The Holy Spirit abides with us always; he is always within us, in our hearts.

—General Audience, St. Peter's Square, April 9, 2014

MARCH 30

SAINTS MICHAEL, GABRIEL, AND RAPHAEL, ARCHANGELS

Michael—which means: "Who is like God?"—is the champion of the primacy of God, of his transcendence and power. Michael . . . defends the People of God from their enemies and above all from the archenemy par excellence, the devil. And Saint Michael triumphs because in him it is God who acts.

—Blessing of Statue of St. Michael the Archangel,
Vatican Gardens, July 5, 2013

SEPTEMBER 29

I would like a question to resound in the hearts of each one of you, and I would like you to answer it honestly: . . . Which idol lies hidden in my life that prevents me from worshipping the Lord? Worshipping is stripping ourselves of our idols, even the most hidden ones, and choosing the Lord as the center, as the highway of our lives.

—Homily, Basilica of St. Paul Outside-the-Walls, April 14, 2013

MARCH 31

SAINT WENCESLAUS; SAINT LAWRENCE RUIZ AND COMPANIONS

"Forgive us our trespasses, as we forgive those who trespass against us." In these words from the Our Father, there is a plan for life, based on mercy.

—Address, Pastoral Visit to the Dioceses of Campobasso-Boiano and Isernia-Venafro, July 5, 2014

SEPTEMBER 28

What does it mean that Jesus is risen? It means that the love of God is stronger than evil and death itself; it means that the love of God can transform our lives and let those desert places in our hearts bloom. The love of God can do this!

—*Urbi et Orbi* Message, Easter Sunday, March 31, 2013

APRIL 1

May we not resist the Holy Spirit but allow him to work in our lives so that he can renew us, the Church and the world.

—Twitter, June 13, 2014

SEPTEMBER 27

SAINT FRANCIS OF PAOLA

Awareness of the marvels that the Lord has wrought
for our salvation disposes our minds and hearts to an
attitude of thanksgiving to God for all that he has given
us, for all that he has accomplished for the good of his
People and for the whole of humanity.

—General Audience, St. Peter's Square,
Ash Wednesday, March 5, 2014

APRIL 2

SAINTS COSMAS AND DAMIAN

We are invited to open ourselves to the light of Christ in order to bear fruit in our lives, to eliminate unchristian behaviors. . . . We must repent of this, eliminate these behaviors in order to journey well along the way of holiness, which has its origin in Baptism.

—Angelus Address, St. Peter's Square,
Fourth Sunday of Lent, March 30, 2014

SEPTEMBER 26

Difficulties and trials are part of the path that leads to God's glory, just as they were for Jesus who was glorified on the cross; we will always encounter them in life! Do not be discouraged! We have the power of the Holy Spirit to overcome these trials!

—Homily, St. Peter's Square, Mass and Conferral of the Sacrament of Confirmation, April 28, 2013

APRIL 3

The forgiveness of our sins is not something we can give ourselves. . . . Forgiveness is not the fruit of our own efforts but rather a gift; it is a gift of the Holy Spirit who fills us with the wellspring of mercy and of grace that flows unceasingly from the open heart of the crucified and risen Christ.

—General Audience, St. Peter's Square, February 19, 2014

SEPTEMBER 25

SAINT ISIDORE

Let us follow Jesus! We accompany, we follow Jesus, but above all we know that he accompanies us and carries us on his shoulders. This is our joy; this is the hope that we must bring to this world. Please do not let yourselves be robbed of hope! Do not let hope be stolen—the hope that Jesus gives us!

—Homily, St. Peter's Square,
Palm Sunday, March 24, 2013

APRIL 4

Love for God is made manifest in Jesus. For we cannot love air. . . . Do we love air? . . . No, no, we cannot; we love people, and the person we love is Jesus, the gift of the Father among us.

—Angelus Address, St. Peter's Square, August 11, 2013

SEPTEMBER 24

The Holy Spirit, gift of the Risen Jesus, conveys divine life
to us and thus lets us enter into the dynamism of the Trinity,
which is a dynamism of love, of communion, of mutual service,
of sharing. A person who loves others for the very joy of
love is a reflection of the Trinity.

—Angelus Address, St. Peter's Square,
Solemnity of the Most Holy Trinity, June 15, 2014

APRIL 5

SAINT PIO OF PIETRELCINA

The Father has given us life; Jesus has given us salvation, he accompanies us, he leads us, he supports us, he teaches us; and the Holy Spirit? What does he give us? He loves us! He gives us love. Let us think of God in this way and ask Our Lady . . . to teach us to understand properly what God is like.

—Homily, Roman Parish of Sts. Elizabeth and Zachariah,
May 26, 2013

SEPTEMBER 23

Sometimes we see things according to our liking or according to the condition of our heart, with love or with hate, with envy. . . . No, this is not God's perspective. Wisdom is what the Holy Spirit works in us so as to enable us to see things with the eyes of God. This is the gift of wisdom.

—General Audience, St. Peter's Square, April 9, 2014

APRIL 6

Let us ask ourselves: . . . what steps are we taking to ensure that faith governs the whole of our existence? We are not Christian "part-time," only at certain moments, in certain circumstances, in certain decisions; no one can be Christian in this way. We are Christian all the time! Totally!

—General Audience, St. Peter's Square, May 15, 2013

SEPTEMBER 22

SAINT JOHN BAPTIST DE LA SALLE

The Eucharist communicates the Lord's love for us: a love so
great that it nourishes us with himself, a freely given love,
always available to every person who hungers and needs to
regenerate his own strength.

—Homily, St. John Lateran Square,
Solemnity of the Most Holy Body and Blood of Christ, June 19, 2014

APRIL 7

SAINT MATTHEW, APOSTLE AND EVANGELIST

The Gospel allows you to know the real Jesus, it lets you know the living Jesus; it speaks to your heart and changes your life. And then, yes, you leave it all. You can effectively change lifestyles, or continue to do what you did before, but you are someone else, you are reborn: you have found what gives meaning.

—Angelus Address, St. Peter's Square, July 27, 2014

SEPTEMBER 21

Christ comes to bring us the mercy of a God who saves. We are asked to trust in him, to correspond to the gift of his love with a good life, made up of actions motivated by faith and love.

—General Audience, St. Peter's Square, April 24, 2013

APRIL 8

Saints Andrew Kim Taegon and Paul Chong Hasang and Companions

Today Christ is knocking at the door of your heart, of my heart. He calls you and me to rise, to be wide awake and alert, and to see the things in life that really matter. What is more, he is asking you and me to go out . . . knocking on the doors of other people's hearts, inviting them to welcome him into their lives.

—Meeting with Asian Youth, Korea, August 15, 2014

SEPTEMBER 20

Jesus tells us that there is a door which gives us access to God's family, to the warmth of God's house, of communion with him. This door is Jesus himself (cf. John 10:9). . . . He is the entrance to salvation. He leads us to the Father, and the door that is Jesus is never closed.

—Angelus Address, St. Peter's Square, August 25, 2013

APRIL 9

SAINT JANUARIUS

What are the relationships like in our parishes, in our
communities? Do we treat each other like brothers and sisters?
Or do we judge one another, do we speak evil of one another,
do we just tend our own vegetable patch? Or do we care for one
another? These are the questions of charity!

—General Audience, St. Peter's Square, October 23, 2013

SEPTEMBER 19

"The Lord set his love upon you and chose you"
(Deuteronomy 7:7). God is bound to us; he chose us,
and this bond is forever, not so much because we are faithful,
but because the Lord is faithful and endures our faithlessness,
our indolence, our lapses.

—Homily, Gemelli Hospital,
Solemnity of the Most Sacred Heart of Jesus, June 27, 2014

APRIL 10

We are called to open ourselves more and more to the action of the Holy Spirit, to offer our unreserved readiness to be instruments of God's mercy, of his tenderness, of his love for every man and every woman and especially for the poor, the outcast, and those who are distant.

—Address to General Directors of Pontifical Missionary Works,
Clementine Hall, May 17, 2013

SEPTEMBER 18

Worshipping the Lord means giving him the place that he must have; worshipping the Lord means stating, believing—not only by our words—that he alone truly guides our lives; worshipping the Lord means that we are convinced before him that he is the only God, the God of our lives, the God of our history.

—Homily, Basilica of St. Paul Outside-the-Walls, April 14, 2013

APRIL 11

SAINT ROBERT BELLARMINE

Being Church means . . . proclaiming and bringing God's salvation into our world, which often goes astray and needs to be encouraged, given hope, and strengthened on the way. The Church must be a place of mercy freely given, where everyone can feel welcomed, loved, forgiven, and encouraged to live the good life of the Gospel.

—Apostolic Exhortation *The Joy of the Gospel,* 114

SEPTEMBER 17

If we entrust our life to [Christ], if we let ourselves be
guided by him, we are certain to be in safe hands,
in the hands of our Savior, of our Advocate.

—General Audience, St. Peter's Square, April 17, 2013

APRIL 12

SAINTS CORNELIUS AND CYPRIAN

Peace is not something which can be bought or sold;
peace is a gift to be sought patiently and to be "crafted" through
the actions, great and small, of our everyday lives. The way
of peace is strengthened . . . if we never forget that we have
the same Father in heaven and that we are all his children,
made in his image and likeness.

—Homily, International Stadium,
Amman, Jordan, May 24, 2014

SEPTEMBER 16

Saint Martin I

Spreading the Gospel means that we are the first to proclaim and live the reconciliation, forgiveness, peace, unity, and love which the Holy Spirit gives us. Let us remember Jesus' words: "By this all men will know that you are my disciples, if you have love for one another" (John 13:35).

—General Audience, St. Peter's Square, May 22, 2013

APRIL 13

OUR LADY OF SORROWS

Let us turn to the Virgin Mary: her Immaculate Heart, a mother's heart, has fully shared in the "compassion" of God, especially in the hour of the passion and death of Jesus. May Mary help us to be mild, humble, and merciful with our brothers.

—Angelus Address, St. Peter's Square, June 9, 2013

SEPTEMBER 15

Why the cross? Because Jesus takes upon himself the evil, the filth, the sin of the world, including the sin of all of us, and he cleanses it; he cleanses it with his blood, with the mercy and the love of God.

—Homily, St. Peter's Square,
Palm Sunday, March 24, 2013

APRIL 14

Exaltation of the Holy Cross

The cross represents all the love of God, which is greater than our iniquities and our betrayals. In the cross we see the monstrosity of man when he allows evil to guide him; but we also see the immensity of the mercy of God, who does not treat us according to our sins but according to his mercy.

—Address, Way of the Cross at the Colosseum, April 18, 2014

SEPTEMBER 14

Jesus, Bread of eternal life, came down from heaven
and was made flesh thanks to the faith of Mary Most Holy. . . .
Let us ask Our Lady to help us rediscover the beauty of the
Eucharist, to make it the center of our life, especially
at Sunday Mass and in adoration.

—Angelus Address, St. Peter's Square,
Solemnity of the Most Holy Body and Blood of Christ, June 22, 2014

APRIL 15

SAINT JOHN CHRYSOSTOM

We are the soil where the Lord tirelessly sows the seed of his word and of his love. . . . Which soil does [our heart] resemble: that of the path, the rocks, the thorns? It's up to us to become good soil with neither thorns nor stones, but tilled and cultivated with care, so that it may bear good fruit for us and for our brothers and sisters.

—Angelus Address, St. Peter's Square, July 13, 2014

SEPTEMBER 13

Let the Risen Jesus enter your life; welcome him as a friend, with trust—he is life! If up till now you have kept him at a distance, step forward. He will receive you with open arms.

—Homily, St. Peter's Basilica,
Easter Vigil, March 30, 2013

APRIL 16

Most Holy Name of Mary

The Holy Virgin made of her existence an unceasing and beautiful gift to God because she loved the Lord. Mary's example is an incentive . . . for all of us to live in charity for our neighbor, not out of some sort of social duty, but beginning from the love of God, from the charity of God.

—Address at Meeting with the Missionaries of Charity at the Homeless Shelter *Dono di Maria*, May 21, 2013

SEPTEMBER 12

God is patient; he knows how to wait. This is so beautiful: our God is a patient father, who always waits for us and waits with his heart in hand to welcome us, to forgive us. He always forgives us if we go to him.

—Angelus Address, St. Peter's Square, July 20, 2014

APRIL 17

Let us open the doors to the Spirit; let ourselves be guided by him and allow God's constant help to make us new men and women, inspired by the love of God which the Holy Spirit bestows on us!

—Homily, St. Peter's Square, Mass and Conferral of the Sacrament of Confirmation, April 28, 2013

SEPTEMBER 11

Unity is a grace for which we must ask the Lord, that he may liberate us from the temptation of division, of conflict between us, of selfishness, of gossip. How much evil gossip does, how much evil! Never gossip about others, never!

—General Audience, St. Peter's Square, June 19, 2013

APRIL 18

Let us all remember this: one cannot proclaim the Gospel of Jesus without the tangible witness of one's life. Those who listen to us and observe us must be able to see in our actions what they hear from our lips and so give glory to God!

—Homily, Basilica of St. Paul Outside-the-Walls, April 14, 2013

SEPTEMBER 10

Hope does not let us down—the hope of the Lord! . . . How often do the expectations we have in our hearts come to nothing! Our hope as Christians is strong, safe, and sound on this earth where God has called us to walk, and it is open to eternity because it is founded on God who is always faithful.

—General Audience, St. Peter's Square, April 10, 2013

APRIL 19

SAINT PETER CLAVER

The Spirit leads us to praise the Lord from the depths of our heart and to recognize, in all that we have and all that we are, an invaluable gift of God and a sign of his infinite love for us.

—General Audience, St. Peter's Square, May 21, 2014

SEPTEMBER 9

We say we must seek God, go to him and ask forgiveness, but when we go, he is waiting for us; he is there first! In Spanish we have a word that explains this well: *primerear*—the Lord always gets there before us; he gets there first, he is waiting for us!

—Address, St. Peter's Square, Vigil of Pentecost
with Ecclesial Movements, May 18, 2013

APRIL 20

NATIVITY OF THE BLESSED VIRGIN MARY

To grow in tender love, and a respectful and sensitive charity, we have a sure Christian model to contemplate: Mary, the Mother of Jesus and our Mother, who is always attentive to the voice of God and the needs and troubles of her children.

—Message for the 22nd World Day of the Sick 2014

SEPTEMBER 8

Saint Anselm

Being the Church, to be the People of God in accordance with the Father's great design of love, means to be the leaven of God in this humanity of ours. It means to proclaim and to bring God's salvation to this world of ours so often led astray [and] in need of answers that give courage, hope, and new vigor for the journey.

—General Audience, St. Peter's Square, June 12, 2013

APRIL 21

Remember, tomorrow [is] the liturgical celebration of the
Nativity of Our Lady. It would be her birthday. And what does
one do when Mama celebrates her birthday? One greets her
with best wishes on her birthday. . . . Tomorrow, remember,
bright and early, from your heart and from your lips, to greet
Our Lady and wish her "Happy Birthday!"

—Angelus Address, St. Peter's Square, September 7, 2014

SEPTEMBER 7

Let us be enveloped by the mercy of God; let us trust in his patience, which always gives us more time. Let us find the courage to return to his house, . . . allowing ourselves to be loved by him and to encounter his mercy in the sacraments.

—Homily, Basilica of St. John Lateran,
Divine Mercy Sunday, April 7, 2013

APRIL 22

The gift of understanding is important for our Christian life. Let us ask it of the Lord, . . . that he may give us all this gift to understand the things that happen as he understands them, and to understand, above all, the word of God in the Gospel.

—General Audience, St. Peter's Square, April 30, 2014

SEPTEMBER 6

SAINT GEORGE; SAINT ADALBERT

The love of Christ, which has blessed and sanctified the union of husband and wife, is able to sustain their love and to renew it when, humanly speaking, it becomes lost, wounded, or worn out. The love of Christ can restore to spouses the joy of journeying together.

—Homily, St. Peter's Square,
Mass with the Rite of Marriage, September 14, 2014

APRIL 23

May we learn to say "thank you" to God and to one another. We teach children to say it, and then we forget to do it ourselves.

—Twitter, March 20, 2014

SEPTEMBER 5

Saint Fidelis of Sigmaringen

What is "the" truth? Can we know it? Can we find it? . . . The truth is not grasped as a thing; the truth is encountered. It is not a possession; it is an encounter with a Person.

—General Audience, St. Peter's Square, May 15, 2013

APRIL 24

Neither our weaknesses, nor our sins, nor the many obstacles that are placed in the way of witnessing and proclaiming the Gospel can hold us back. The experience of an encounter with the Lord is what spurs us on and gives us the joy of announcing him to all peoples.

—Address to the Pontifical Mission Societies,
Clementine Hall, May 9, 2014

SEPTEMBER 4

SAINT MARK, EVANGELIST

The Church is a people who serves God. . . . Above all, we are *a people who serve God*. Service to God is realized in different ways, in particular in prayer and in adoration, in proclaiming the Gospel and in the testimony of love.

—Homily, Pastoral Visit to the Dioceses
of Campobasso-Boiano and Isernia-Venafro, July 5, 2014

APRIL 25

SAINT GREGORY THE GREAT

God does not hide himself from those who seek
him with a sincere heart, even though they do so
tentatively, in a vague and haphazard manner.

—Apostolic Exhortation *The Joy of the Gospel,* 71

SEPTEMBER 3

Sinners we may be, but Jesus forgives us. Let us hear that voice of Jesus who, by the power of God, says to us: "Come out! Leave that tomb you have within you. Come out. I give you life, I give you happiness, I bless you, I want you for myself."

—Homily, Roman Parish of San Gregorio Magno,
April 6, 2014

APRIL 26

We must all ask ourselves: how do I let myself be guided by the Holy Spirit in such a way that my life and witness of faith is both unity and communion? Do I convey the word of reconciliation and of love, which is the Gospel, to the milieus in which I live? . . . Do I create unity around me? Or do I cause division by gossip, criticism, or envy?

—General Audience, St. Peter's Square, May 22, 2013

SEPTEMBER 2

This is the culmination of the Gospel, it is the Good News par excellence: Jesus, who was crucified, is risen! This event is the basis of our faith and our hope.

—*Urbi et Orbi* Message, Easter Sunday, April 20, 2014

APRIL 27

"Please," "thank you," and "sorry." With these three words, with the prayer of the husband for the wife and vice versa, by always making peace before the day comes to an end, marriage will go forward. The three magic words, prayer, and always making peace.

—General Audience, St. Peter's Square, April 2, 2014

SEPTEMBER 1

SAINT LOUIS GRIGNION DE MONTFORT; SAINT PETER CHANEL

"Come to me, all who labor and are heavy laden, and I will give you rest" (Matthew 11:28). . . . Jesus addresses this invitation: "Come to me." Jesus' invitation is for everyone —but especially for those who suffer the most.

—Angelus Address, St. Peter's Square, July 6, 2014

APRIL 28

We believe in the Risen One who conquered evil and death! . . . The resurrection of Christ is our greatest certainty; he is our most precious treasure! How can we not share this treasure, this certainty with others? It is not only for us; it is to be passed on, to be shared with others.

—General Audience, St. Peter's Square, April 3, 2013

AUGUST 31

SAINT CATHERINE OF SIENA

When someone is summoned by the judge or is involved in legal proceedings, the first thing he does is to seek a lawyer to defend him. We have One who always defends us, who defends us from the snares of devil, who defends us from ourselves and from our sins!

—General Audience, St. Peter's Square, April 17, 2013

APRIL 29

The salvation which God offers us is the work of his mercy. No human efforts, however good they may be, can enable us to merit so great a gift. God, by his sheer grace, draws us to himself and makes us one with him.

—Apostolic Exhortation *The Joy of the Gospel*, 112

AUGUST 30

SAINT PIUS V

Let us show the joy of being children of God, the freedom that living in Christ gives us, which is true freedom, the freedom that saves us from the slavery of evil, of sin, and of death!

—General Audience, St. Peter's Square, April 10, 2013

APRIL 30

Passion of Saint John the Baptist

As "precursor" and "witness," John the Baptist plays a role central to the entire Scripture. . . . With his witness, John points us to Jesus, invites us to follow him, and tells us without mincing his words that this requires humility, repentance, and conversion; it is an invitation that calls for humility, repentance, and conversion.

—General Audience, Paul VI Audience Hall, August 6, 2014

AUGUST 29

SAINT JOSEPH THE WORKER

In the silence of the daily routine, Saint Joseph, together with Mary, shares a single common center of attention: Jesus. They accompany and nurture the growth of the Son of God made man for us with commitment and tenderness.

—General Audience, St. Peter's Square, May 1, 2013

MAY 1

Do not be afraid of Confession! When one is in line to go to Confession, one feels all these things, even shame, but then when one finishes Confession, one leaves free, grand, beautiful, forgiven, candid, happy. This is the beauty of Confession!

—General Audience, St. Peter's Square, February 19, 2014

AUGUST 28

When we see the love that God has for us,
we feel the desire to draw close to him: this is conversion.

—General Audience, St. Peter's Square,
Ash Wednesday, March 5, 2014

MAY 2

SAINT MONICA

How many prayers that holy mother [Monica] raised to God for her son [Augustine], and how many tears she shed! I am thinking of you, dear mothers, how often you pray for your children, never tiring! Continue to pray and to entrust them to God. . . . Knock at God's heart with prayers for your children.

—General Audience, St. Peter's Square, September 18, 2013

AUGUST 27

Do not be afraid to cast yourselves into the arms of God;
whatever he asks of you, he will repay a hundredfold.

—Twitter, July 11, 2014

MAY 3

A witness to the Gospel is one who has encountered Jesus Christ, who knows him, or better, who feels known by him, recognized, respected, loved, forgiven; and this encounter has deeply touched him, filled him with a new joy, given life a new meaning. And this shines through; it's passed on to others.

—Address to Apostolic Movement of the Blind and the Little Mission for the Deaf and Mute, Paul VI Hall, March 29, 2014

AUGUST 26

The Christian should be a luminous person; one who brings light, who always gives off light! A light that is not his, but a gift from God, a gift from Jesus. We carry this light. . . . It is truly God who gives us this light, and we must give it to others. Shining lamps! This is the Christian vocation.

—Angelus Address, St. Peter's Square, February 9, 2014

MAY 4

In intimacy with God and in listening to his word, little by little we put aside our own way of thinking, which is most often dictated by our closures, by our prejudice and by our ambitions, and we learn instead to ask the Lord: "What is your desire? What is your will? What pleases you?"

—General Audience, St. Peter's Square, May 7, 2014

AUGUST 25

To remember what God has done and continues to do for me, for us, to remember the road we have traveled; this is what opens our hearts to hope for the future. May we learn to remember everything that God has done in our lives.

—Homily, St. Peter's Basilica,
Easter Vigil, March 30, 2013

MAY 5

Saint Bartholomew, Apostle

Let us ask the Lord for this grace: that our hearts become free and filled with light so that we can rejoice as children of God.

—Twitter, August 21, 2014

AUGUST 24

When we welcome the Holy Spirit into our hearts and allow him to act, Christ makes himself present in us and takes shape in our lives; through us, it will be he—Christ himself—who prays, forgives, gives hope and consolation, serves the brethren, draws close to the needy and to the least, creates community and sows peace.

—General Audience, St. Peter's Square, January 29, 2014

MAY 6

<small>SAINT ROSE OF LIMA</small>

The Spirit leads us into the divine life as true
children of God, as sons and daughters in the
only-begotten Son, Jesus Christ. Are we open to the
Holy Spirit? Do we let ourselves be guided by him?

—Homily, St. Peter's Square,
Mass for *Evangelium Vitae* Day, June 16, 2013

AUGUST 23

Let's not be afraid to cross the threshold of faith in Jesus, to let him enter our life more and more, to step out of our selfishness, our closure, our indifference to others so that Jesus may illuminate our life with a light that never goes out.

—Angelus Address, St. Peter's Square, August 25, 2013

MAY 7

QUEENSHIP OF THE BLESSED VIRGIN MARY

Mary, woman of listening, open our ears; grant us to know how to listen to the word of your Son Jesus among the thousands of words of this world; grant that we may listen to the reality in which we live, to every person we encounter, especially those who are poor, in need, in hardship.

—Address at the Conclusion of the Marian Month of May, St. Peter's Square, May 31, 2013

AUGUST 22

Marriage is also an everyday task, I could say a craftsman's task, a goldsmith's work, because the husband has the duty of making the wife more of a woman and the wife has the duty of making the husband more of a man. Growing also in humanity, as man and woman. . . . Always act so that the other may grow.

—Address to Engaged Couples Preparing for Marriage,
St. Peter's Square, February 14, 2014

MAY 8

SAINT PIUS X

God's word is unpredictable in its power. The Gospel speaks of a seed which, once sown, grows by itself, even as the farmer sleeps (Mark 4:26-29). The Church has to accept this unruly freedom of the word, which accomplishes what it wills in ways that surpass our calculations and ways of thinking.

—Apostolic Exhortation *The Joy of the Gospel*, 22

AUGUST 21

Let us allow ourselves to be guided by the Holy Spirit;
let us allow him to speak to our hearts and say this to
us: God is love, God is waiting for us, God is Father;
he loves us as a true father loves; he loves us truly, and
only the Holy Spirit can tell us this in our hearts.

—General Audience, St. Peter's Square, May 8, 2013

MAY 9

When families bring children into the world, train them in faith and sound values, and teach them to contribute to society, they become a blessing in our world. Families can become a blessing for all of humanity!

—Meeting with Families, Mall of Asia Arena, Manila, January 16, 2015

AUGUST 20

I cannot imagine a Christian who
does not know how to smile.
May we joyfully witness to our faith.

—Twitter, January 30, 2014

MAY 10

SAINT JOHN EUDES

Enthusiasm is contagious. But do you know where this word comes from, enthusiasm? It comes from the Greek and it means "to have something of God inside" or "to be inside God." Enthusiasm, when it is healthy, demonstrates this: that one has something of God inside and expresses him joyously.

—Address to Young People of the Dioceses of
Abruzzi and Molise, July 5, 2014

AUGUST 19

Let us remember this in our lives as Christians: God always waits for us, even when we have left him behind! He is never far from us, and if we return to him, he is ready to embrace us.

— Homily, Basilica of St. John Lateran,
Divine Mercy Sunday, April 7, 2013

MAY 11

God's face is the face of a merciful father who is always patient. Have you thought about God's patience, the patience he has with each one of us? That is his mercy. He always has patience, patience with us; he understands us, he waits for us, he does not tire of forgiving us if we are able to return to him with a contrite heart.

—Angelus Address, St. Peter's Square, March 17, 2013

AUGUST 18

Saints Nereus and Achilleus; Saint Pancras

If we think we don't need God who reaches out to us through Christ because we believe we can make do on our own, we are headed for a fall. God alone can truly save and free us.

—Message for Lent 2014

MAY 12

Wake up!"—This word speaks of a responsibility which the Lord gives you. It is the duty to be vigilant, not to allow the pressures, the temptations, and the sins of ourselves or others to dull our sensitivity to the beauty of holiness, to the joy of the Gospel.

—Homily, Mass for the 6th Asian Youth Day,
Korea, August 17, 2014

AUGUST 17

OUR LADY OF FATIMA

Blessed Virgin Mary of Fatima, . . . guard our life with your embrace: bless and strengthen every desire for good; give new life and nourishment to faith; sustain and enlighten hope; awaken and animate charity; guide us all on the path to holiness.

—Act of Entrustment to Mary, Virgin of Fatima,
St. Peter's Square, October 13, 2013

MAY 13

Jesus wants us free. And where is this freedom created? It is created in dialogue with God in the person's own conscience. If a Christian is unable to speak with God, if he cannot hear God in his own conscience, he is not free; he is not free.

—Angelus Address, St. Peter's Square, June 30, 2013

AUGUST 16

SAINT MATTHIAS, APOSTLE

How does the Lord find our hearts? A heart that is firm
as a rock, or a heart like sand, that is doubtful, diffident,
disbelieving? . . . If the Lord finds in our heart, I don't say a
perfect, but sincere, genuine faith, then he also sees in us living
stones with which to build his community. This community's
foundation stone is Christ.

—Angelus Address, St. Peter's Square, August 24, 2014

MAY 14

Assumption of the Blessed Virgin Mary

Mary's Assumption shows us our own destiny as God's adoptive children and members of the body of Christ. Like Mary our Mother, we are called to share fully in the Lord's victory over sin and death and to reign with him in his eternal kingdom. This is our vocation.

—Homily, Apostolic Journey to the Republic of Korea, August 15, 2014

AUGUST 15

SAINT ISIDORE THE FARMER

To be a saint is not a luxury. It is necessary for the salvation of the world. This is what the Lord is asking of us.

—Homily, St. Peter's Basilica,
Mass with New Cardinals, February 23, 2014

MAY 15

Saint Maximilian Kolbe

Those who know Jesus, encounter him personally, are captivated, attracted by so much goodness, so much truth, so much beauty, and all with great humility and simplicity. To seek Jesus, to find Jesus: this is the great treasure!

—Angelus Address, St. Peter's Square, July 27, 2014

AUGUST 14

"Peace be with you" (John 20:19, 21, 26). This is not a greeting, nor even a simple good wish; it is a gift, indeed, the precious gift that Christ offered his disciples after he had passed through death and hell.

—Regina Caeli Address, St. Peter's Square, April 7, 2013

MAY 16

SAINTS PONTIAN AND HIPPOLYTUS

Only by behaving as children of God, without despairing at our shortcomings, at our sins; only by feeling loved by him will our lives be new, enlivened by serenity and joy. God is our strength! God is our hope!

—General Audience, St. Peter's Square, April 10, 2013

AUGUST 13

Pray always, but not in order to convince the Lord by dint of words! He knows our needs better than we do! Indeed, persevering prayer is the expression of faith in a God who calls us to fight with him every day and at every moment in order to conquer evil with good.

—Angelus Address, St. Peter's Square, October 20, 2013

MAY 17

SAINT JANE FRANCES DE CHANTAL

Peace is not simply the absence of war, but "the work of
justice" (cf. Isaiah 32:17). And justice, as a virtue, calls for
the discipline of forbearance; it demands that we not forget
past injustices but overcome them through forgiveness,
tolerance, and cooperation.

—Address to Authorities, Apostolic Journey to the Republic of Korea,
August 14, 2014

AUGUST 12

SAINT JOHN I

To listen to the Lord, we must learn to contemplate, feel his constant presence in our lives, and we must stop and converse with him, give him space in prayer. Each of us . . . should ask ourselves, "How much space do I give to the Lord? Do I stop to talk with him?"

—General Audience, St. Peter's Square, May 1, 2013

MAY 18

SAINT CLARE OF ASSISI

If we do not pray, we will not know the most important thing of all: God's will for us. And for all our activity, our busy-ness, without prayer we will accomplish very little.

—Meeting with Families, Mall of Asia Arena,
Manila, January 16, 2015

AUGUST 11

Remain steadfast in the journey of faith, with firm hope in the Lord. This is the secret of our journey! He gives us the courage to swim against the tide . . . to go against the current; this is good for the heart, but we need courage to swim against the tide. Jesus gives us this courage!

—Homily, St. Peter's Square, Mass and Conferral of the Sacrament of Confirmation, April 28, 2013

MAY 19

SAINT LAWRENCE

If we listen to the Holy Spirit, . . . he endows us with wisdom, which is seeing with God's eyes, hearing with God's ears, loving with God's heart, directing things with God's judgment. This is the wisdom the Holy Spirit endows us with, and we can all have it. We only have to ask it of the Holy Spirit.

—General Audience, St. Peter's Square, April 9, 2014

AUGUST 10

SAINT BERNARDINE OF SIENA

This is the great work of Jesus today in heaven: showing the Father the price of forgiveness, his wounds. This is the beauty that urges us not to be afraid to ask forgiveness; the Father always pardons, because he sees the wounds of Jesus, he sees our sin and he forgives it.

—Regina Caeli Address, St. Peter's Square, June 1, 2014

MAY 20

SAINT TERESA BENEDICTA OF THE CROSS (EDITH STEIN)

In the end we will all be judged by the same measure with which we have judged: the mercy we have shown to others will also be shown to us. Let us ask Our Lady, our Mother, to help us to grow in patience, in hope, and in mercy with all brothers and sisters.

—Angelus Address, St. Peter's Square, July 20, 21014

AUGUST 9

SAINT CHRISTOPHER MAGALLANES AND COMPANIONS

Lord, we pray to you for all the peoples of the earth: you who have conquered death, grant us your life, grant us your peace!

—*Urbi et Orbi* Message, Easter Sunday, April 20, 2014

MAY 21

SAINT DOMINIC

Jesus loves us definitively; he has chosen us definitively; he gave himself to each of us definitively. He is our defender and big brother and will be our only judge. How beautiful it is to be able to face life's ups and downs in Jesus' company, to have his Person and his message with us!

—Address to Young People of the Dioceses of Abruzzi and Molise, July 5, 2014

AUGUST 8

Saint Rita of Cascia

Whoever experiences divine mercy is impelled to be an architect of mercy among the least and the poor. In these "littlest brothers," Jesus awaits us (cf. Matthew 25:40); let us receive mercy and let us give mercy!

—Homily, St. Peter's Basilica,
Communal Reconciliation Service, March 28, 2014

MAY 22

SAINT SIXTUS II AND COMPANIONS; SAINT CAJETAN

Our Christian witness is authentic when
it is faithful and unconditional.

—Twitter, September 4, 2014

AUGUST 7

The Eucharist is the summit of God's saving action: the Lord Jesus, by becoming bread broken for us, pours upon us all of his mercy and his love so as to renew our hearts, our lives, and our way of relating with him and with the brethren.

—General Audience, St. Peter's Square, February 5, 2014

MAY 23

TRANSFIGURATION OF THE LORD

Jesus manifests himself, and by his Transfiguration he invites us to gaze at him. And looking at Jesus purifies our eyes and prepares them for eternal life, for the vision of heaven.

—Homily, Roman Parish of Santa Maria dell' Orazione,
March 16, 2014

AUGUST 6

May the Virgin Mary help us to be docile to the Holy Spirit,
so that we may be able to esteem one another and converge
ever more deeply in faith and love, keeping our hearts
open to the needs of our brothers.

—Regina Caeli Address, St. Peter's Square, May 18, 2014

MAY 24

DEDICATION OF THE BASILICA OF SAINT MARY MAJOR IN ROME

Let us look to [Mary], and allow her to look upon us, for she is our mother and she loves us so much; let us allow ourselves to be watched over by her so that we may learn how to be . . . more courageous in following the word of God.

—Angelus Address, St. Peter's Square, December 8, 2013

AUGUST 5

SAINT BEDE THE VENERABLE; SAINT GREGORY VII;
SAINT MARY MAGDALENE DE' PAZZI

In faith, let us invoke the Spirit, the Lord and Giver of Life, that
he may renew the face of the earth, be a source of healing for
our wounded world, and reconcile the hearts of all men and
women with God the Creator.

—Address to the Catholicos of the Cilicia of the Armenians,
Clementine Hall, June 5, 2014

MAY 25

Now is the time to say to Jesus: "Lord, I have let myself be deceived; in a thousand ways I have shunned your love, yet here I am once more, to renew my covenant with you. I need you. Save me once again, Lord, take me once more into your redeeming embrace."

—Apostolic Exhortation *The Joy of the Gospel,* 3

AUGUST 4

Saint Philip Neri

I would like to ask everyone a question: how many of you pray every day to the Holy Spirit? There will not be many, but we must fulfill Jesus' wish and pray every day to the Holy Spirit, that he open our heart to Jesus.

—General Audience, St. Peter's Square, May 15, 2013

MAY 26

We are all called to receive with an open mind and heart the word of God which the Church imparts every day, because this word has the capacity to change us from within. . . . The word of God which Mother Church gives us transforms us, makes our humanity pulse, not according to mundane flesh, but according to the Holy Spirit.

—General Audience, St. Peter's Square, September 3, 2014

AUGUST 3

If I let myself be touched by the grace of the Risen Christ,
if I let him change me in that aspect of mine which is not good,
which can hurt me and others, I allow the victory of Christ
to be affirmed in my life, to broaden its beneficial action.
This is the power of grace!

—Regina Caeli Address, St. Peter's Square, April 1, 2013

MAY 27

SAINT EUSEBIUS OF VERCELLI; SAINT PETER JULIAN EYMARD

Faith is not simply an individual decision which takes place in the depths of the believer's heart, nor a completely private relationship between the "I" of the believer and the divine "Thou," between an autonomous subject and God. By its very nature, faith is open to the "We" of the Church; it always takes place within her communion.

—Encyclical *The Light of Faith*, 39

AUGUST 2

Money must serve, not rule! The Pope loves everyone, rich and poor alike, but he is obliged in the name of Christ to remind all that the rich must help, respect, and promote the poor. I exhort you to generous solidarity and to the return of economics and finance to an ethical approach which favors human beings.

—Apostolic Exhortation *The Joy of the Gospel*, 58

MAY 28

SAINT ALPHONSUS LIGUORI

Jesus tells us in the Gospel that being Christians does not
mean having a "label"! . . . Being Christian is living and
witnessing to faith in prayer, in works of charity,
in promoting justice, in doing good.

—Angelus Address, St. Peter's Square, August 25, 2013

AUGUST 1

Ours is a joy born not of having many possessions but from having encountered a Person: Jesus, in our midst. It is born from knowing that with him we are never alone, even at difficult moments, even when our life's journey comes up against problems and obstacles that seem insurmountable, and there are so many of them!

—Homily, St. Peter's Square, Palm Sunday, March 24, 2013

MAY 29

SAINT IGNATIUS OF LOYOLA

The love of Jesus Christ lasts forever; it has no end because it is the very life of God. This love conquers sin and gives the strength to rise and begin again, for through forgiveness the heart is renewed and rejuvenated.

—Homily, St. Peter's Basilica,
Communal Reconciliation Service, March 28, 2014

JULY 31

The Holy Spirit teaches us to see with the eyes of Christ, to live life as Christ lived, to understand life as Christ understood it. . . . What does the Holy Spirit tell us? He says: God loves you. He tells us this: God loves you, God likes you.

—General Audience, St. Peter's Square, May 8, 2013

MAY 30

SAINT PETER CHRYSOLOGUS

The one who listens attentively to the word of God and truly prays always asks the Lord: what is your will for me?

—Twitter, May 19, 2014

JULY 30

Visitation of the Blessed Virgin Mary to Elizabeth

Immediately after having received the news from the Angel and having conceived Jesus, Mary sets out in haste to go and help her elderly relative Elizabeth. And thus she reveals that the privileged path to serve God is to serve our brothers and sisters in need.

—Homily, Pastoral Visit to the Dioceses of Campobasso-Boiano and Isernia-Venafro, July 5, 2014

MAY 31

SAINT MARTHA

Think about this: when we go to confess our weaknesses,
our sins, we go to ask the pardon of Jesus, but we also go to
renew our Baptism through his forgiveness. . . . Confession
is not a matter of sitting down in a torture chamber; .
rather it is a celebration.

—General Audience, St. Peter's Square, November 13, 2013

JULY 29

SAINT JUSTIN

May the Church be a place of God's mercy and hope, where all feel welcomed, loved, forgiven, and encouraged to live according to the good life of the Gospel. And to make others feel welcomed, loved, forgiven, and encouraged, the Church must be with doors wide open so that all may enter.

— General Audience, St. Peter's Square, June 12, 2013

JUNE 1

This is the work of the Holy Spirit: he brings us the new things of God. He comes to us and makes all things new; he changes us. . . . God is even now making all things new; the Holy Spirit is truly transforming us, and through us he also wants to transform the world in which we live.

—Homily, St. Peter's Square, Mass and Conferral of the Sacrament of Confirmation, April 28, 2013

JULY 28

SAINTS MARCELLINUS AND PETER

The death and resurrection of Jesus are the heart of our hope. . . . It is the resurrection itself that opens us to greater hope, for it opens our life and the life of the world to the eternal future of God, to full happiness, to the certainty that evil, sin, and death may be overcome.

—General Audience, St. Peter's Square, April 3, 2013

JUNE 2

Jesus is the one who is sent forth, filled with the Spirit of the Father. Anointed by the same Spirit, we also are *sent* as messengers and witnesses of peace. The world has much need of us as messengers of peace, witnesses of peace! The world needs this. The world asks us to bring peace and to be a sign of peace!

—Homily, International Stadium,
Amman, Jordan, May 24, 2014

JULY 27

SAINT CHARLES LWANGA AND COMPANIONS

When a person truly knows Jesus Christ and believes in him, that person experiences his presence in life as well as the power of his resurrection, and cannot but communicate this experience.

—Regina Caeli Address, St. Peter's Square, April 14, 2013

JUNE 3

SAINTS JOACHIM AND ANNE, PARENTS OF THE BLESSED VIRGIN MARY

Today is the Feast of Saint Anne, whom I like to call "Jesus' grandma," and today is a beautiful day to celebrate grandmothers. . . . Saint Anne is the woman who prepared her daughter to become queen, to become queen of heaven and earth. This woman did a good job!

—Homily, Park of the Royal Palace of Caserta, Italy, July 26, 2014

JULY 26

God constantly surprises us; he bursts our categories, he wreaks havoc with our plans. And he tells us: trust me, do not be afraid; let yourself be surprised, leave yourself behind and follow me!

—Homily, St. Peter's Square, Marian Day on the Occasion of the Year of Faith, October 13, 2013

JUNE 4

SAINT JAMES, APOSTLE

The Church needs credible lay witnesses to the saving truth
of the Gospel, its power to purify and transform human hearts,
and its fruitfulness for building up the human family in unity,
justice, and peace. We know there is but one mission of
the Church of God, and that every baptized Christian
has a vital part in this mission.

—Address to the Leaders of the Apostolate of the Laity,
Klottonngnae, Korea, August 16, 2014

JULY 25

SAINT BONIFACE

The mission of the Holy Spirit, in fact, is to beget harmony—
he is himself harmony—and to create peace in different
situations and between different people. Diversity of ideas
and persons should not trigger rejection or prove an
obstacle, for variety always enriches.

—Homily, International Stadium,
Amman, Jordan, May 24, 2014

JUNE 5

Saint Sharbel Makhluf

The mystery of [Jesus'] voice is evocative. Only think that from our mother's womb we learn to recognize her voice and that of our father. . . . Jesus' voice is unique! If we learn to distinguish it, he guides us on the path of life, a path that goes beyond even the abyss of death.

—Regina Caeli Address, St. Peter's Square, April 21, 2013

JULY 24

Saint Norbert

Let us pray for Christians who are victims of persecution
so that they know how to respond to evil with good.

—Twitter, March 6, 2014

JUNE 6

SAINT BRIDGET OF SWEDEN

Now, Lord, come to our aid! Grant us peace, teach us peace; guide our steps in the way of peace. Open our eyes and our hearts, and give us the courage to say: "Never again war!"; "With war everything is lost." Instill in our hearts the courage to take concrete steps to achieve peace.

—Invocation for Peace, Vatican Gardens, June 8, 2014

JULY 23

Carry the Gospel of Jesus Christ everywhere, even to those most de-Christianized, especially in the margins of life. Evangelize with love, bring God's love to all. . . . May you be messengers and witnesses of the infinite goodness and inexhaustible mercy of the Father.

—Address to Representatives of the Neocatechumenal Way,
Paul VI Audience Hall, February 1, 2014

JUNE 7

God's faithfulness is stronger than our
unfaithfulness and our infidelities.

—Twitter, September 10, 2014

JULY 22

Sometimes we may be tempted to give in to laziness,
or worse, to discouragement, especially when faced with
the hardships and trials of life. In these cases, . . . let us invoke
the Holy Spirit so that through the gift of fortitude, he may lift
our heart and communicate new strength and enthusiasm to
our life and to our following of Jesus.

—General Audience, St. Peter's Square, May 14, 2014

JUNE 8

SAINT LAWRENCE OF BRINDISI

When our eyes are illumined by the Spirit, they open to
contemplate God, in the beauty of nature and in the grandeur
of the cosmos, and they lead us to discover how everything
speaks to us about him and his love. All of this arouses in us
great wonder and a profound sense of gratitude!

—General Audience, St. Peter's Square, May 21, 2014

JULY 21

The Holy Spirit *teaches us:* he is the Interior Master. He guides us along the right path, through life's challenges. He teaches us the path, the way. In the early times of the Church, Christianity was called "the way" (cf. Acts 9:2), and Jesus himself is the Way. The Holy Spirit teaches us to follow him, to walk in his footprints.

—Homily, St. Peter's Basilica,
Solemnity of Pentecost, June 8, 2014

JUNE 9

SAINT APOLLINARIS

A marriage is not successful just because it endures; quality is important. . . . The Lord can multiply your love and give it to you fresh and good each day. He has an infinite reserve! He gives you the love that stands at the foundation of your union, and each day he renews and strengthens it.

—Address to Engaged Couples Preparing for Marriage,
St. Peter's Square, February 14, 2014

JULY 20

People today certainly need words, but most of all they need us to bear witness to the mercy and tenderness of the Lord, which warms the heart, rekindles hope, and attracts people towards the good. What a joy it is to bring God's consolation to others!

—Homily, St. Peter's Basilica, Mass with Seminarians, Novices, and Those Discerning Their Vocations, July 7, 2013

JUNE 10

The sacraments express and realize an effective and profound communion among us, for in them we encounter Christ the Savior and, through him, our brothers and sisters in faith. The sacraments are not mere appearances, they are not rituals; they are the power of Christ—Jesus Christ is present in the sacraments.

—General Audience, St. Peter's Square, November 6, 2013

JULY 19

SAINT BARNABAS, APOSTLE

Jesus on the cross feels the whole weight of the evil, and with the force of God's love he conquers it, he defeats it with his resurrection. This is the good that Jesus does for us on the throne of the cross.

—Homily, St. Peter's Square,
Palm Sunday, March 24, 2013

JUNE 11

Saint Camillus de Lellis

No one is the most important person in the Church; we are all equal in God's eyes. Some of you might say, "Listen, Mr. Pope, you are not our equal." Yes, I am like each one of you; we are all equal, we are brothers and sisters!

—General Audience, St. Peter's Square, June 26, 2013

JULY 18

It is the Spirit himself whom we received in Baptism, who teaches us, who spurs us to say to God, "Father," or rather, "Abba!" which means "Papa" or ["Dad"]. Our God is like this: he is a dad to us. The Holy Spirit creates within us this new condition as children of God.

—General Audience, St. Peter's Square, April 10, 2013

JUNE 12

"Peace I leave with you; my peace I give to you; not as the world gives do I give to you" (John 14:27). This peace is the fruit of the victory of God's love over evil; it is the fruit of forgiveness. And it really is like this: true peace, that profound peace, comes from experiencing God's mercy.

—Regina Caeli Address, St. Peter's Square, April 7, 2013

JULY 17

Saint Anthony of Padua

There is never a reason to lose hope. Jesus says:
"I am with you until the end of the world."

—Twitter, June 19, 2014

JUNE 13

OUR LADY OF MOUNT CARMEL

Our Lady is always close to us; she looks upon each one of us
with maternal love and accompanies us always on our journey.
Do not hesitate to turn to her for every need, especially when
the burden of life with all its problems makes itself felt.

—Address to Sri Lankan Community in Italy,
St. Peter's Basilica, February 8, 2014

JULY 16

When we draw near with tender love to those in need of care, we bring hope and God's smile to the contradictions of the world. When generous devotion to others becomes the hallmark of our actions, we give way to the Heart of Christ and bask in its warmth, and thus contribute to the coming of God's kingdom.

—Message for the 22nd World Day of the Sick 2014

JUNE 14

SAINT BONAVENTURE

Nothing is lost with God, but without him everything is lost;
open your hearts to him and trust in him, and your eyes will
see his ways and his splendor (cf. Proverbs 23:26).

—Phone Call to Participants in the 39th Pilgrimage
from Macerata to Loreto, June 7, 2014

JULY 15

God is not only at the origin of love, but in Jesus Christ
he calls us to imitate his own way of loving: "As I have loved you,
that you also love one another" (John 13:34). To the extent to
which Christians live this love, they become credible
disciples of Christ to the world.

—Homily, St. Peter's Basilica,
Communal Reconciliation Service, March 28, 2014

JUNE 15

Saint Kateri Tekakwitha

The Lord in his great goodness and his infinite mercy always takes us by the hand lest we drown in the sea of our fears and anxieties. He is ever at our side; he never abandons us. And so, let us not be overwhelmed by fear or [become] disheartened, but with courage and confidence, let us press forward in our journey and in our mission.

—Address, Church of Gethsemane,
Pilgrimage to the Holy Land, May 26, 2014

JULY 14

Popular piety highly values symbols, and the heart of Jesus is the ultimate symbol of God's mercy. But it is not an imaginary symbol; it is a real symbol which represents the center, the source from which salvation flowed for all of humanity.

—Angelus Address, St. Peter's Square, June 9, 2013

JUNE 16

SAINT HENRY

Celebrating the Sacrament of Reconciliation means
being enfolded in a warm embrace: it is the embrace of
the Father's infinite mercy. . . . I am telling you: each time
we go to Confession, God embraces us. God rejoices!
Let us go forward on this road.

—General Audience, St. Peter's Square, February 19, 2014

JULY 13

Dear friends, be glad! . . . Don't be afraid of joy! That joy which
the Lord gives us when we allow him to enter our life. Let
us allow him to enter our lives and invite us to go out to the
margins of life and proclaim the Gospel. Don't be afraid of joy.
Have joy and courage!

—Angelus Address, St. Peter's Square, July 7, 2013

JUNE 17

When we seek [Jesus], we discover that he is waiting to welcome us, to offer us his love. And this fills your heart with such wonder that you can hardly believe it, and this is how your faith grows—through encounter with a Person, through encounter with the Lord.

—Address, St. Peter's Square, Vigil of Pentecost
with Ecclesial Movements, May 18, 2013

JULY 12

This is a prayer we must pray every day: "Holy Spirit, make my heart open to the word of God, make my heart open to goodness, make my heart open to the beauty of God every day."

—General Audience, St. Peter's Square, May 15, 2013

JUNE 18

Being a disciple means being constantly ready to bring the love of Jesus to others, and this can happen unexpectedly and in any place: on the street, in a city square, during work, on a journey.

—Apostolic Exhortation *The Joy of the Gospel*, 127

JULY 11

SAINT ROMUALD

May the Virgin Mary, perfect creation of the Trinity, help us to make our whole lives, in small gestures and more important choices, a homage to God, who is Love.

—Angelus Address, St. Peter's Square,
Solemnity of the Most Holy Trinity, June 15, 2014

JUNE 19

Evangelizing is the Church's mission. It is not the mission of only a few, but it is mine, yours, and our mission. The apostle Paul exclaimed, "Woe to me if I do not preach the Gospel!" (1 Corinthians 9:16). We must all be evangelizers, especially with our life!

—General Audience, St. Peter's Square, May 22, 2013

JULY 10

How do we live our being Church? Are we living stones or are we, as it were, stones that are weary, bored, or indifferent? . . . A Christian like that is all wrong; the Christian must be alive, rejoicing in being Christian; he or she must live this beauty of belonging to the People of God which is the Church.

—General Audience, St. Peter's Square, June 26, 2013

JUNE 20

Saint Augustine Zhao Rong and Companions

All of us are journeying towards the heavenly Jerusalem,
the ultimate newness which awaits us and all reality,
the happy day when we will see the Lord's face—
that marvelous face, the most beautiful face of the
Lord Jesus—and be with him forever, in his love.

—Homily, St. Peter's Square, Mass and Conferral
of the Sacrament of Confirmation, April 28, 2013

JULY 9

SAINT ALOYSIUS GONZAGA

I like to think that a synonym, another name that we Christians could be called, is this: we are men and women, we are a people who bless. The Christian by his life must bless always, bless God and bless all people. We Christians are a people who bless, who know how to bless. This is a beautiful vocation!

—General Audience, St. Peter's Square, June 18, 2014

JUNE 21

We have to pray, together as Catholics and also with other Christians; pray that the Lord give us the gift of unity, unity among us. . . . Seek unity, the unity that builds the Church. Unity comes from Jesus Christ. He sends us the Holy Spirit to create unity.

—General Audience, St. Peter's Square, June 19, 2013

JULY 8

Every Christian can witness to God in the workplace, not only
with words, but above all with an honest life.

—Twitter, May 30, 2014

JUNE 22

Our Father never tires of loving, and his eyes never grow weary of watching the road to his home to see if the son who left and was lost is returning. We can speak of God's hope: our Father expects us always; he doesn't just leave the door open to us, but he awaits us.

—Homily, St. Peter's Basilica,
Communal Reconciliation Service, March 28, 2014

JULY 7

Let us ask the Lord, each of us, for eyes that know how to see beyond appearance; ears that know how to listen to cries, whispers, and also silence; hands able to support, embrace, and minister. Most of all, let us ask for a great and merciful heart that desires the good and salvation of all.

—Address to the Italian Catholic Action,
Paul VI Audience Hall, May 3, 2014

JUNE 23

We are called . . . to become rest and comfort for our brothers and sisters, with a docile and humble attitude, in imitation of the Teacher. Docility and humility of heart help us not only to take on the burden of others, but also to keep our personal views, our judgments, our criticism, or our indifference from weighing on them.

—Angelus Address, St. Peter's Square, July 6, 2014

JULY 6

NATIVITY OF SAINT JOHN THE BAPTIST

[John the Baptist] is the "precursor," the one who prepares
the coming of the Lord, preparing the people to convert
the heart to receive God's comfort already at hand. . . .
He makes us recognize in Jesus the One who comes from
on High, to forgive our sins and to make of his people
his Bride, the first fruits of the new humanity.

—General Audience, Paul VI Audience Hall, August 6, 2014

JUNE 24

SAINT ELIZABETH OF PORTUGAL; SAINT ANTHONY ZACCARIA

The great threat in today's world is the loneliness
of hearts oppressed by greed.

—Twitter, July 22, 2014

JULY 5

Ever since we were children, our parents have taught us to start and end the day with a prayer, to teach us to feel that the friendship and the love of God accompanies us. Let us remember the Lord more in our daily life!

—General Audience, St. Peter's Square, May 1, 2013

JUNE 25

To live the experience of faith means to allow oneself to be nourished by the Lord and to build one's own existence not with material goods but with the reality that does not perish: the gifts of God, his word and his body.

—Homily, St. John Lateran Square,
Solemnity of the Most Holy Body and Blood of Christ, June 19, 2014

JULY 4

Holiness is a vocation for everyone. Thus we are all called to walk on the path of holiness, and this path has a name and a face: the face of Jesus Christ. He teaches us to become saints.

—Angelus Address, St. Peter's Square, Solemnity of All Saints, November 1, 2013

JUNE 26

Saint Thomas, Apostle

"My Lord and my God!" With this simple yet faith-filled invocation, [Thomas] responds to Jesus' patience. He lets himself be enveloped by divine mercy; he sees it before his eyes, in the wounds of Christ's hands and feet and in his open side, and he discovers trust: he is a new man, no longer an unbeliever, but a believer.

—Homily, Basilica of St. John Lateran,
Divine Mercy Sunday, April 7, 2013

JULY 3

SAINT CYRIL OF ALEXANDRIA

The joy of the Gospel fills the hearts and lives of all who encounter Jesus. Those who accept his offer of salvation are set free from sin, sorrow, inner emptiness and loneliness. With Christ joy is constantly born anew.

—Apostolic Exhortation *The Joy of the Gospel,* 1

JUNE 27

The Church is the salt of the earth; she is the light of the world. She is called to make present in society the leaven of the kingdom of God, and she does this primarily with her witness, the witness of brotherly love, of solidarity, and of sharing with others.

—Address, St. Peter's Square, Vigil of Pentecost
with Ecclesial Movements, May 18, 2013

JULY 2

SAINT IRENAEUS

Remember what Saint Paul says: "What shall I boast of,
if not my weakness, my poverty?" (cf. 2 Corinthians 11:30).
Precisely in feeling my sinfulness, in looking at my sins,
I can see and encounter God's mercy, his love,
and go to him to receive forgiveness.

—Homily, Basilica of St. John Lateran,
Divine Mercy Sunday, April 7, 2013

JUNE 28

SAINT JUNÍPERO SERRA

When we let ourselves to be guided by the Holy Spirit, he brings us to harmony, unity, and respect for various gifts and talents. Have you understood well? No gossiping, no envy, no jealousy! Understood?

—Regina Caeli Address, St. Peter's Square, May 18, 2014

JULY 1

SAINTS PETER AND PAUL, APOSTLES

God is always capable of transforming us too, the way he transformed Peter and Paul; transforming the heart and forgiving us for everything, thus transforming the darkness of our sin into a dawn of light. God is like this: he transforms us, he always forgives us, as he did with Peter and as he did with Paul.

—Angelus Address, St. Peter's Square,
Solemnity of Sts. Peter and Paul, June 29, 2014

JUNE 29

FIRST MARTYRS OF THE HOLY ROMAN CHURCH

The legacy of the martyrs can inspire all men and women
of good will to work in harmony for a more just, free, and
reconciled society, thus contributing to peace and the protection
of authentically human values in our world.

—Homily at Mass for the Beatification of Korean Martyrs,
Seoul, August 16, 2014

JUNE 30